Saint Jerome

SAINT JEROME

BY

Régine and Madeleine Pernoud

TRANSLATED BY

Rosemary Sheed

THE MACMILLAN COMPANY

A Division of The Crowell-Collier Publishing Company

NEW YORK 1962

270 B
Jerome PES

Nihil obstat
    Donald A. Panella, M.A., S.T.L., S.S.L.
    CENSOR DEPUTATUS

Imprimatur
    ✠ Francis Cardinal Spellman
      ARCHBISHOP OF NEW YORK
January 22, 1962

The Macmillan Company, New York
Brett-Macmillan Ltd., Galt, Ontario

Printed in the United States of America

Library of Congress catalog card number: 62-13438

Contents

To Jerome and Emmanuel

1

Saint Jerome in Art

Few of the saints in the calendar have received so much attention from painters and miniaturists as St. Jerome. A complete survey of all the works devoted to him would be a history of Western art in itself. He is to be found in the oldest manuscripts of the early Middle Ages; the scenes of his life figure particularly in the "Bible of Charles the Bald" (early ninth century).[1] This was because his life, as we shall see, was closely bound up with the study of the Bible which

[1] This work is Number 1 in the *Bibliothèque nationale* in Paris (*fonds latin*).

was at that time, and indeed throughout the Middle Ages, *the* book *par excellence.* The most precious, most exquisitely illuminated manuscripts were dedicated to him, and the love people had for the Scriptures attached itself also to the figure of Jerome.

He was also to receive that halo of legend that inevitably forms round the heads of all the striking personalities of history. Indeed one might also say that without the seal of folklore, which alone marks the entry of any figure into the world of popular acclaim, the seal of history is incomplete.

St. Jerome's popularity was expressed by a mass of legendary attributes which gradually became inseparable from his appearance: there was the cardinal's hat, the stone with which, as a withered old man kneeling in the desert, he beat his breast, and of course the inevitable lion, lying at his feet.

We may, however, note that the earliest miniatures do not have this equipment demanded by the legends. In particular, those in Charles the Bald's bible show us St. Jerome on his journeys, pursuing his Hebrew studies, instructing his nuns, or handing out work to his copyists, and are thus wholly accurate. But the Lives of St. Jerome by pious hagiographers were not content with historical accuracy. Early in the seventh century one of them had spoken of him as "cardinal priest"—that is to say, priest of one of the churches of Rome; this was enough to result, as years went on, in his being made a cardinal in the sense in which we use the word today, a dignitary of the Roman Church, attributing to him the title of Sancta Anastasia;[2] henceforward, the famous hat was there to stay.

As for the desert, and the stone with which he beat his breast, these are details which illustrate very strikingly how history grows into legend, and how legend should not be despised in the name of history: St. Jerome did in fact live in the desert, and it was he who introduced asceticism to the West. His character and his holiness are better expressed by this gesture immortalized by painters from some unknown fifteenth-century artist to Titian and Leonardo, than they could be by any long verbal account.

On the other hand, it is a pity that these, like most other painters of St. Jerome, depict him as a permanently old man. This is indeed an unforgivable historical error: when he arrived in the desert, St. Jerome was twenty-eight; he stayed there only two years and a half, so that he was barely thirty when he returned to Antioch. Thus he was a young man in his prime when he embraced asceticism and gave such an example of penance. The tendency to picture him as an old man grew chiefly out of an error over his date

[2] We know that at the beginning the name of cardinal priest, in other words, principal priest, was given to anyone in charge of a Roman parish. Later the name cardinal was given to those prelates called to make up the Pope's council, and assure the papal elections. As a reminder of the title's origin, each of these was given the title of a parish in Rome.

of birth. Modern scholarship has made Jerome sixteen years younger by giving this date as 347, instead of 331. When he died, therefore (at the end of 419 or beginning of 420), he was not in his nineties, as had been thought.

As for the lion, that certainly represents an incursion of legend into history, an incursion quite uncalled for, and only based on St. Jerome's having spent time in the desert. However, the *Golden Legend* shows him accompanied by a lion, and the passage is well worth quoting:

"One evening," says Jacobus de Voragine's text, "while Jerome was seated with his brethren to listen to sacred reading, a lion came limping into the monastery. All the brethren at once fled: Jerome alone went to meet him, as to a guest, and when the lion had shown him its wounded paw, he called some of the brethren, and ordered them to wash its wound and take care of it. They did; and the lion, cured, stayed among the brethren like a domestic animal. Jerome therefore took counsel with his brethren, and commanded the lion to take to pasture and guard a donkey of theirs which they used for carrying wood. This it did. The lion was an excellent shepherd, always ready to protect the donkey, and never failing to bring it back to the monastery at mealtimes. But one day, when the lion was asleep, some merchants with camels who were going past, saw a donkey by itself, and quickly took possession of it." What was the consternation of the monks when the lion returned alone to the monastery, with its tail between its legs: had it eaten the donkey? For its penance, "they gave the lion the donkey's work to do, using it to carry their wood; the animal did it with exemplary patience. But one day, when it had finished its work, it began to run across the fields, and saw in the distance some merchants with camels, with a donkey going ahead to lead the way, as the custom was in that country. The lion at once hurled itself upon the caravan with a dreadful roaring, making the merchants flee; then, striking the ground with its tail, it made the camels come back with it to the monastery." Jerome and the other monks recognized their donkey, and shortly afterward the contrite merchants came to admit their theft, while the lion was feasted magnificently.

Legends of this kind were spread by the hundreds, from mouth to mouth, among the monks of the East, and also among the pilgrims who visited them. This one certainly has no closer connection with fact than the linking of a lion with a period of living in the desert—a tenuous one to say the least. There is probably also a confusion with the legend of St. Gerasimus. Yet this habit of using a completely imaginary story to decorate the bleak desert scene would certainly not have displeased Jerome himself; for one of the first things he ever wrote had as its theme a visit to the desert, and he allowed himself to embroider upon it as his imagination suggested. This was his *Life of*

St. Paul the first hermit, which Jerome wrote during his retirement in the desert of Chalcis around the year 376, and in which he also summarizes oral traditions handed down among the monks of Egypt and Syria. A certain Paul of Thebes, during the persecution of Decius or Valerian, had fled to the desert, and finally sought refuge in a cave which had previously been used as a workshop by counterfeiters. He lived there, for nearly a century, a life of continual prayer in absolute solitude. A stream that flowed near his cave supplied him with water; a palm tree that shadowed it supplied him with clothes; his food was brought to him every day by a crow, which brought a piece of bread in its beak and laid it at the hermit's feet. Paul of Thebes was 112 when he received his first visitor: St. Anthony, who had also lived in solitude for sixty-five years, was one day tempted to pride—he believed himself to be the most perfect of monks because he was the most solitary. The next night, a revelation from God told him that another monk, older, more solitary, and more perfect, was living in an even more remote desert; so, the next morning, St. Anthony took his stick, and set out to find this exemplary ascetic.

And it is clear from Jerome's description of that journey how little he minded mixing legend with history: Anthony met with a centaur on his way, and then a satyr—no doubt suggested by the famous accounts of St. Anthony's temptations, which so many painters and decorators have since immortalized.

The morning of the third day, Anthony at last came to the cave of Paul of Thebes; the two hermits greeted each other as friends, and that day, in honor of the visitor, the crow left a double ration of bread. Then, at Paul's invitation, Anthony returned to his hermitage to get the cloak that his bishop, St. Athanasius, had given him. When he got back, Paul had died, and in an ecstatic vision, Anthony saw him going up to heaven, surrounded by a choir of angels. He then wrapped Paul's body in the cloak, and just as he was wondering how he could summon the strength to dig a grave for the saintly hermit, two lions ran up, and scratching at the earth with their claws had soon made a trench, in which Anthony laid him.

It would be a mistake to believe that Paul of Thebes did not exist; he was worshiped in Egypt at the end of the fourth century. But from what were simply oral traditions, Jerome constructed a wonderful story, which is moving to read even today.

In doing so, he has shown us one of the essential traits of his personality, one of the richest of all time. Often as we think of Jerome the ascetic, the scholar, the exegete, let us not forget Jerome the poet.

7

2

The Age in Which Jerome Lived

S t. Jerome was born in the year 347. As one of his recent biographers[1] points out, by the mere fact of saying so we pay homage to a number of scholars whose researches made it possible to establish this fact, for it had long been thought that he was born fifteen or sixteen years earlier.

He was born at Stridon in Dalmatia, at the extreme northeast of Italy, and thus one of the farthest points of the Roman Empire. His family was Christian.

Being born into a Christian family in the Roman

[1] Paul Monceaux.

Empire in the middle of the fourth century did not mean being set upon any well defined path, religiously speaking. Fifty years earlier, things were much more clear-cut; to be born a Christian meant to be born into the risk of martyrdom. Indeed, we know that the most violent of all the persecutions were those in the reign of Diocletian (284-305). But at the period when St. Jerome entered the world, the Church was free. The Edict of Milan in 313 had given it the freedom of the city. The Emperor looked favorably upon it; Constantine asked for baptism before he died, and from then on the Church became a recognized institution; it had three centuries of existence behind it—more than the faithful needed to make them feel they were following an established tradition; indeed, there were already a number who had settled down into luke-warmness. Jerome's parents were among them; they thought it sufficient to go on feast days to assist at the ceremonies in the church at Aquileia to which they belonged. It is curious, at this distance, to think that a creature like Jerome, so ardent and enthusiastic, so quick to anger, so demonstrative both in friendship and in invective, could have been born in any such tepid surroundings.

It was not that there were no occasions of controversy in the society of that time. Few periods present such a variety of features as were shown by that astounding century. To start with, even to be a Christian might mean one of several things—a partisan of

9

Athanasius, or Arius, a partisan of Pelagius, or the
Lucifer who, his name notwithstanding, was a most
intransigent Catholic, more Catholic than the Pope.
It was a time indeed when heresies ran riot. Though
it may be described as a Christian world under the
aegis of the Empire, it must be added that many of
those very Christians were teaching heresy, founding
sects, and breaking away from the Church. Africa,
where Christianity was extremely prosperous, had been
torn by the Donatist schism, which declared every sin-
ner already damned, and therefore to be cut off from
the society of believers; it had its own well organized
church, complete with bishops and an autonomous
hierarchy. It had been in existence for over a century
by now, and Donatists were to storm Catholic churches.

Above all, there was Arianism, whose influence on
the Christian world of that time can be compared only
to that of Protestantism in modern times. Arius, a
priest from the East, living in Alexandria, taught what
amounted to a denial of the Incarnation: Christ was
simply a creature, and was not therefore God like the
Father, but merely a kind of hero who merited the
special favor of God. Arius' heresy was not slow to
spread, and its influence was commensurate with the
personal prestige of its author. Indeed in 325, the
Council of Nicaea—the first Council since the eman-
cipation of the Church—was called to consider his
theses. It was there that the Nicene Creed was formu-
lated (which we still say at Mass), which reaffirmed

the solemn statement of the dogma of the Incarnation
in the Apostles' Creed. This was a great date in the
Church's history, this first ecumenical council that
brought together all the Christian bishops of East
and West (three hundred and eighteen, according to
St. Athanasius). Among them were men who bore
marks of torture they had undergone under Licinius,
who had continued to persecute in the East even after
the Edict of Milan.

But the Council did not put an end to the heresy;
in spite of being condemned by the Church, Arianism
spread amazingly fast. And Christianity was placed
in a critical position by the fact that the Barbarians,
like the Goths, were converted from paganism to
Arianism. When these peoples, Visigoths, Ostrogoths,
Burgundians, Vandals, and so on, poured into the
Empire, it was a question of converting not pagans,
but heretics—a very much harder task: not virgin
soil, but a field already planted with weeds. The
Arian heresy did not finally disappear till the sixth
century, and huge areas of Christendom fell prey to
it—all the Germanic lands, northern Italy, Illyria, and
a number of countries in the East.

It looked as though the Church, only now allowed
to show itself by daylight, was at once going to
collapse into fragments, to break up into a multitude
of warring sects.

Nor was this the worst danger it faced in that
century of turmoil. The fact that, until then, it had

11

lived a semiclandestine life, sometimes tolerated, sometimes persecuted by the state, had given it one advantage, though a negative one; its position in relation to the state was clearly defined, since the state always remained more or less hostile. But, from the moment of his recognizing the existence of the Church, even before himself becoming a Christian, Constantine displayed an officious interest in Christian affairs. As early as 316, he entered the Donatist controversy. And it was he who summoned the bishops to the Council of Nicaea, to pronounce upon the teachings of Arius. Nothing could be more disturbing than such an intrusion of lay power into matters that were strictly religious. One of Constantine's successors, Constantius, was to go so far as to declare: "In questions of faith, my will is the law."[2]

The Church had to enter into that hard apprenticeship, never ending for the Christian, which teaches how "to render to Caesar the things that are Caesar's, and to God the things that are God's." In every age it must find a solution as best it can that suits the situation; and in the time immediately after Constantine, the shadow of that first Christian emperor certainly fell heavily upon it. One of his successors, Valens, having been won over to Arianism, persecuted those who were not Arianists, and in later years, the Germanic emperors of the Middle Ages never stopped in-

[2] For all this, see Daniel-Rops, *L'Eglise des apôtres et des martyrs,* particularly pp. 463 ff.

12

terfering in Church affairs, appointing bishops, and even Popes as it suited them. And, on the other hand, the Church developed a dangerous habit of having recourse to the "secular arm," to the temporal power, to carry out her discipline, punish heresy, and so on. In other words, a new phase was beginning: henceforward, the Church must face the test of life out in the world. Emerging from a tortured and imprisoned childhood, it must now undergo the crisis of growing up. But Christ had, after all, spoken of struggles that would continue throughout its existence and be resolved only with his second coming.

As yet all the inhabitants of the Empire were far from won over to Christianity. Though better known, it had not become any more convincing. At the time of St. Jerome, many informed minds were not ill-disposed to the teaching of Christ, but felt it to be "largely outdated." This again we may note as a permanent feature of the Church's life through the ages: there will always be those who consider its doctrine as "largely outdated" by modern progress, whether scientific, philosophical, technological, or what have you. In the fourth century, serious thinkers considered that, though He had undoubtedly shed valuable light, Christ had merely opened the way to a higher doctrine, too elevated for the great mass of men, and attainable only by a few initiates. Some among them were content simply to be philosophers; these were the Gnostics who, as early as the second century, had

13

emptied Christ's teaching of everything living and concrete, and drawn from it simply abstract speculation.

Far more alarming were to be the Manicheans. They were the disciples of a kind of Magus, born in Persia and called Manes who, in the third century, claimed to have brought mankind "the definitive religion" (Daniel-Rops). It was made up of a compound of oriental religions, Buddhism and others, of Greek philosophy and Christian doctrines, but preponderantly of the old pagan cult in force since Zoroaster's day, which saw the world as the work of two principles, a god of good and a god of evil. The first gave light, the soul, spiritual life; the second carnal life, matter, the body. The Manichean system made Christ an incarnation of the god of good, who would continue to struggle on earth with the god of evil up to the point when, everyone having agreed to lead a perfect life (in other words to abstain from all further procreation), this would bring the world to an end. Manichean teachings were condemned as much by some of the greatest pagan philosophers, like Plotinus, as by Christians like St. Cyril of Jerusalem. Yet, in the fourth century, they had given rise to a complete church, with bishops and prophets. Even St. Augustine was, for a time in his youth, a believer, and as late as the Middle Ages, this same Manichean heresy reappeared in the form of Albigensianism.

Thus there were occasions in plenty for discussion, and indeed for impassioned polemic, in the fourth century. For those who remained convinced pagans, the bitterest reproach they made to the Church was that it was preaching Utopias—that slavery must disappear, for instance, appeared at that time unthinkable. Further, with its dangerous novelties, it was bringing about the loss of the culture inherited from Greece which was the glory of the Roman empire. Indeed, if there ever was a "quarrel between old and new," it took place in this age when St. Jerome was born, and he was destined to play an astonishing part in it. With horror, people saw buildings going up in Rome itself which were in total disharmony with the canons of classic art, which were thought to be the very Code of Beauty.

The places where Christians met and worshiped were at first simply the private houses of individuals—there were reckoned to be twenty-five parishes in Rome in the second century. By now, however, nothing remained of these. They had been gradually deserted for the catacombs, which became the only safe places to hold ceremonies in time of persecution. When, after 313, it became possible to build churches, it would have been logical to make them follow the style of the old temples; after all, those who built them had the most perfect models before them to copy. Trajan's forum, in Rome, was still new, with its majestic porticos around a rectangular space, perfectly proportioned, and the whole city was like a museum, with its innumerable statues and triumphal columns— the column of Trajan, the column of Marcus Aurelius with its imposing friezes of bas-reliefs of Roman victories. Sculpture was, in fact, far and away the favorite art of the Greco-Latin world.

Logically, therefore, as I say, one might have expected to see a new crop of temples, ornamented like the rest with statues and bas-reliefs, but with scenes from the Gospel instead of battle scenes, busts of bishops instead of emperors.

But, while the architecture of the earliest Roman basilicas remained close to the style to which people were accustomed, there was an almost total absence of sculpture. Everyone was amazed to see these new temples being covered entirely with mosaics, in the most barbarous colors—glass mosaics, sparkling with red, gold, and blue—a complete contrast with classical mosaic, which made use of only three colors, black, white, and reddish-brown. Mosaic took the place in these new basilicas which painting had held in the catacombs; for, curiously enough, even in these subterranean refuges, the Christians had taken up an art of color, rather than of shape or relief, and the catacombs—or at least some of them—were entirely covered in frescoes.

The connoisseurs of the old art were still further irritated to find that with these new mosaics, as in the catacomb paintings, the canons of academic art had disappeared. Artists took strange liberties with the laws of anatomy and perspective; they did not seem to care whether they represented the human body accurately; they seemed unable to copy the models of which Alexandrine painting (official art, in other words) was so proud.

In short, Romans were witnessing a complete corruption of art—this at least was the opinion of those who understood the matter, and from whom the emperors continued to order the statues for their palaces. Constantine himself, when he was decorating the forum of Byzantium, which was a copy of those in Rome, had had bronze statues made, some of which, however, were Christian in theme—for one represented the Good Shepherd, and another Daniel in the lions' den. But from the beginning, the Christian churches showed an entirely new conception of art: from now on, the role of art was not to represent the material world, but to *animate* the building, in the etymological sense of the word, to give it a soul. Therefore color, which signified life, was far more stressed than the cult of form in which academic art had so gloried. And rather than placing all that color in small pictures like those we have today, or like those found in Roman villas at the time, it was made to cover the whole edifice. What had been born in the catacombs was nothing less than a new aesthetic, as the few mosaics which remain from the fourth century bear witness (these, for instance, in the nave

17

of St. Mary Major, or St. Constance and St. Pudenti-
anna).[3]

This was an avant-garde art whose daring could
hardly fail to scandalize eyes accustomed to the classic
conceptions of aesthetics. In St. Mary Major, for
instance, they saw the mosaicists upsetting all the
laws of perspective by picturing the altar built by
Abraham as a rectangle growing smaller as it came
toward the spectator—as though the painter had
somehow got inside his picture; things in the fore-
ground were smaller than those behind. Instead of
depicting figures in mass, they were heavily outlined
in black with a total disregard for the third dimension.
The cry went up that this was barbarism, with its
ignorance of the laws of art. These Christians, with
their subversive teachings, were imperiling all the
advantages of civilization. Thus the last practicing
pagans, deeply conscious of the importance of this
battle over sacred art, desperately upheld classical
aesthetics. The neo-Platonists, among others, whose
philosophy had certain affinities with Christianity,
made themselves the unremitting defenders of Greco-
Roman art, however decadent it might be. And when
a pagan emperor once more came to the throne of
Caesar—Julian the Apostate, who made the last attempt to revive a paganism then in its death throes—

[3] Anyone interested in this question will find all the details
in *Les Mosaïques chrétiennes* by Van Berchem and Clouzot,
Paris, 1924.

an offensive was launched in the form of a return to busts, statues, and bas-reliefs in the old style. But Christianity, the youth of the world, was to triumph with this new form of artistic expression; beyond its early splendors in Rome, and their copies in Byzantium, it grew and blossomed into our own medieval art.

From now on Byzantium was to be Constantinople. One more great work with which we must credit the fourth century is the founding of a town, a capital of the Empire; this was an enterprise which we may well, *mutatis mutandis,* compare with the founding of Brasilia in our own time. From a simple small town, magnificently situated, it is true, on the straits of the Bosphorus, Constantine's decision was to make a powerful city, a new capital—for the whole eastern Empire—calling for a tremendous labor force. Forty thousand slaves worked under the command of specialists from all over the world. Constantine, with his perhaps somewhat unbalanced genius, created in a few years a city which was for its date enormous; the wall around it was $4\frac{1}{3}$ miles long, its water supply kept in enormous cisterns and brought by an aqueduct that is still used today to supply the inhabitants of Istanbul. In the year 330, on May 11, the fantastic capital was opened, with feasting that lasted for forty days.

3

Youth

Read only what is worth remembering. I will tell you what is essential: the author of the Iliad, the works of the delightful Menander, the cadenced poems of Horace, the harmonious majesty of Virgil; Terence who honors Latin by the elegance of his style . . . ; the crime of Catiline, the civil war of Lepidus, the events and life of Rome after Lepidus and Catullus and the years following . . . the foreign war, with the civil struggles fomented by Sertorius, that complicated it. . . ."

This is the program which the poet Ausonius set out

for his grandson at the end of his teaching career—a glorious one because he had been called upon to be tutor to the Emperor's son. Ausonius, originally from Bordeaux, but a Roman by adoption, was roughly contemporary with St. Jerome; he was only a few years older, for he was born in 335, and he died in 393. This program, then, is likely to have been the same as that followed by the young Jerome, when he came, with his constant friend Bonosus (probably a native of Stridon like himself) to lodge in Rome and follow a course of what we should call secondary studies.

Of his earliest childhood we know almost nothing, except that he spent it at Stridon with his father Eusebius, and his mother whose name we do not even know. From his letters, we learn that he had a grandmother whom he loved dearly, and a certain Aunt Castorina—a formidable character it would seem, to judge by a letter he wrote as an adult, in which he speaks of renewing the attempt he had made a year earlier, without success, to become reconciled with her.

His writings were also to evoke his beloved grandmother, and his games in the slaves' quarters with his friends, particularly Bonosus. It was the life of an only child—he had a sister ten or twelve years younger than himself, and a brother Paulinian, younger still—in a wealthy home. There is nothing out of the ordinary in the memories he has left us

of his childhood. He admitted later in letters that he
had been rather greedy.

"It is a long time! Home, father and mother, sister,
family, and, harder still, the habit of eating well—all
this I gave up for the kingdom of heaven," he wrote.
And he tells how, like other children, he pulled away
his hand to avoid the master's cane—he took, in other
words, the same path as schoolboys of every generation.
We can picture him as one of those children we
see on Roman steles, playing ball, or holding wax
tablets in their hands. These tablets, like the slates
of later years, were used to teach children the rudi-
ments of writing and arithmetic: the soft wax was
held in a slightly hollowed-out piece of wood, and
the child wrote with a kind of stiletto, one end of
which was spatulate for rubbing out. Only later, when
he had acquired some skill, was anyone allowed to
write on expensive materials, like papyrus, or, more
rarely still, parchment, which did not come into general use till the early Middle Ages.

The schoolboy's first years were spent under the
direction of a grammarian; it must have been around
359 that Jerome went, with his inseparable companion
in both play and study, Bonosus, to Rome, to follow
the usual course of initiation into classical literature.
Though we know almost nothing of his earliest years
—those spent at the equivalent of our high school—
we have some details about the next period. The life
of students in Rome in the fourth century was closely

supervised by the authorities. There were police rules to govern their conduct; they had to declare their identity and address and what studies they were following to the magistrates (the equivalent of our police headquarters); they were permitted to stay till the age of twenty, after which they were asked or made to leave—and they might be sent away sooner if there were the slightest breath of scandal, or hint of debauchery.

Jerome was not above enjoying the distractions of Rome; he went to the theater, the circuses, and less respectable places as well; he was later to recall the follies of his youth with remorse. However, they did not prevent his being a brilliant and industrious student. He soaked himself in Virgil and Cicero, acquired a knowledge of Greek which he was to deepen enormously later, and was initiated into the rhetorical exercises that formed the major part of a student's training at that time. For the traditional classical education was directed toward the making of orators. Life was in fact dominated by lawyers and politicians; the study of law was one of the most highly thought of, and every good Roman prided himself on his knowledge of codes and statutes. Jerome describes how he practiced making speeches on subjects set by the masters, along with the rest. These exercises would be artificial disputes in which two students took part in a carefully planned controversy, setting out their arguments in splendid language. Later in life, he said, he used sometimes to dream that he was a student, and that he had been told to deliver an oration—a nightmare that still made him quake, even in old age: "When I awoke," he admitted, "I would be overjoyed to have escaped the ordeal of practicing my oratory."

Of his masters, he spoke particularly of the famous Donatus, a grammarian whom the commentaries were to continue quoting as an authority for several centuries. He also recalled, though he had not been his pupil, the great rhetor of the time, Victorinus, who had a statue put up in his honor during his lifetime. His was the interesting case of a man remaining for a long time faithful to paganism, who was suddenly converted, and from then on as zealous in defending the church as he had been in attacking it. This zeal caused him to be suspended by the Emperor Julian who, in 362, forbade all Christians to teach.

Jerome tells us that he frequented the Athenaeum; this was a place open to the public where one could go to hear lectures and advocacy. But it seems that from this time on, though he still appreciated the polemical contests in which he was himself so skilled, his chief preoccupation was building up his library, rushing to copy every book he could lay hands on. For at that time there was no other way: scroll by scroll one must copy out any book one wanted to possess.

On Sundays, however, one of his favorite pastimes was to visit the catacombs. They had been deserted only fifty years, and were thus an object of pious curiosity, and seem to have made a vivid impression on Jerome: "An occasional light from above here and there lessened the horror of that darkness; it was not so much a window as an opening which let the daylight through. And then one went on again into the blackest darkness, stepping carefully." We can easily picture him with his friends, Rufinus, Helioderus, and the faithful Bonosus, going in single file past the tombs—for which, a few years later, Pope Damasus was to have inscriptions made. Indeed he may even have known Damasus on this first visit to Rome.

At this time Jerome was not yet baptized. This was not necessarily because of the religious tepidity of his parents; the custom of delaying baptism till one was an adult was fairly widespread. It seems, though, that his piety was aroused by seeing daily the devotion of the people of Rome. He was to recall this fact in later years with some emotion: "Rightly is the faith of the Roman people praised. Where else does one find such devout throngs, such numbers of people in the churches and at the tombs of the martyrs?" Therefore, in the year 366, he decided that he too would enter his name for baptism. Preparation for it was made during Lent. The Lateran basilica is thought to have been the place where the seven "scrutinies" took place—seven sessions at which the catechumens were both instructed and examined in doctrinal knowledge. At the third scrutiny some of the preparatory rites took place—the breathing, the anointing of the ears, nostrils and breast.

The most solemn scrutiny took place on Wednesday of the fourth week of Lent, a few days before Passion Sunday; the catechumens came forward in two lines, one of men, one of women, for the bishop to mark the sign of the cross on their foreheads, place his hand on their heads, put some salt in their mouths, and give them his blessing. They were then sent out, and while the congregation sang the Introit, the acolyte, at the door, called each catechumen by name; he returned into the church, accompanied by his godfather or godmother, and was present for the reading of the two Epistles which still occurred in the Mass in those days; then followed the ceremony of anointing the ears, and then after the Gospel, the catechumens once more went out, for only the baptized Christians at that time assisted at Mass.

The final preparations were made on Maundy Thursday, when the catechumen was bathed, and Good Friday, when he fasted until the solemn vigil of Holy Saturday, which has recently been revived in our own liturgy. Dressed in white, the catechumens entered the baptistry of the Lateran; they solemnly renounced Satan, as we still do when we renew our profession of faith. The bishop laid hands on each candidate, and then proceeded to the exorcisms and anointings; each declared his adherence to the Apostles' Creed, then, at cockcrow, each in turn went down

26

to the font with the help of his godparent. It was then the custom to strengthen the newly baptized after their long fasting and vigil by giving them a mixture of milk and honey to drink; later this was made more substantial by the addition of ground almonds—the origin of the custom still found in some places in France of handing round sugared almonds at baptisms.

Jerome was to write later of the mystery that took place in him that Easter night: "We first turned toward the setting sun to renounce all that died in us with sin, and then, turning to the east, we allied ourselves with the Sun of justice, whom we promised to follow in the future." During the week that followed, the newly baptized kept on their white garments, which they wore to the ceremonies of the Easter octave.

This ceremony also coincided, for Jerome and his friend Bonosus, with the end of their student life. Naturally both felt the need of some relaxation, and they decided to travel to Gaul. Gaul was at that time the great country for tourists; it was also the place for good food; its inns were famous, and, according to one traveler of the time, their good living was so cheap that one paid a lump sum, rather than paying for each meal. Jerome cannot fail to have felt the attraction of this, for though baptized, he had not yet been converted to asceticism. He and Bonosus were, in addition, planning to go as far as Trêves, which was more or less the capital of the western empire; they felt that there they might well make contacts that would prove useful for their future careers, for, like all young Romans of the time, they hesitated between politics and the law. Full of hopes and schemes, then, one July day in 367, the friends left Rome.

4

Conversion

That their trip to Gaul was of decisive importance for the two young men was not the result of the gastronomic or touristic delights they found there, nor yet to the series of contacts they were able to make for the future. A totally different contact awaited them.

They certainly must have found many pleasures on their journey, for their upbringing and schooling had prepared them to appreciate what they saw. We do not know their itinerary, but it is almost certain that they went through Lyons, that great city upon which all the strategic roads of the Empire converged. A wholly Roman creation, it had been for three hundred years the scene of a gathering on the first of August of delegates from all the cities of Gaul, met together to offer sacrifice in honor of the emperor on the hill of the Croix-Rousse, where the altar to Rome and Augustus stood; this was always an occasion for splendid ceremonies designed to impress, and to support the imperial propaganda. But to Jerome and Bonosus, it must have been primarily a city of illustrious martyrs—St. Pothinus and St. Blandina, the old bishop and the young slave, both thrown with their companions to the beasts, whose courage in the face of torment is described in a well known letter that has come down to us.

They may also have gone up the Saône valley, which was a route used from the earliest times; they may have passed through Autun where the Romans, as a counter to the old Gallic city of Bibracte, which they had ordered the inhabitants to leave, had made a university, an active center of "Romanization," where orators and politicians were trained. They finally reached the banks of the Moselle, celebrated by Ausonius, and entered Trêves, that vast entrenched camp, that military and strategic center—almost certainly by the Porta Nigra, which still stands today.

On the way, Jerome, who was already interested in the linguistic studies that were to become his major preoccupation, noted the Gallic speech, still living on in the French countryside—even today traces of it remain in agricultural terminology. Later he was to be surprised to find that same speech existed among the Galatians in Asia Minor, despite the fact that it was centuries since they had had any connections with Gaul proper.

Trêves was, at that time, a military city; but strange meetings could sometimes occur in military cities. The Roman legions were really made up of soldiers from all parts of the Empire, and there were many Christians among them, bearing the gospel message all over the world ruled by Rome. It is a striking thought that the immense network of strategic roads that the Roman armies so carefully laid out for their military needs were also the roads chosen for the gospel to travel.

Quite close to Trêves, some more than usually fervent Christians had transplanted the monastic life of the east; St. Athanasius of Alexandria had spent some time in exile there, and had certainly left his imprint in the form of monks who lived as ascetics in little huts. St. Augustine tells how, one day, two officers from the imperial palace were out strolling with the girls they were going to marry, and chanced to enter one of these little huts; they began talking with the hermit who lived there, and when they came out it was to go and consecrate themselves to God.

Was it something like this that happened to Jerome and Bonosus? All we know is that when they returned to Stridon after their journey to Gaul, each told his family that he was no longer interested in politics or government. They had decided to become monks.

One can imagine what an uproar this caused—certainly in Jerome's case. This eldest son, who had been given the most advanced education, for whom they must have cherished the highest ambitions—and justifiably, considering his brilliance! Jerome had, in fact, to leave his family. He must, however, have had great joy in seeing his young brother, and still more his sister, whom he loved so dearly. As we shall see, he was later to exercise a tremendous influence on them both.

He went to live at Aquileia, not far from Stridon, where he also found Bonosus, who had probably encountered the same difficulties at home. Aquileia was at that time the most important port on this part of the Adriatic; it was also a center of commerce and literature, but its chief charm, for Bonosus and Jerome, lay in the presence of a priest, Chromatius, who practised the ascetic ideal that so attracted them. What is curious is that Aquileia, like Trêves, had been a refuge for St. Athanasius of Alexandria, who had spent most of his life in exile; it would seem that in every place where he settled monastic life had taken root.

In those days there was still a very strong sense of the position of bishops—as successors of the apostles; then, as now, the bishop would delegate some of his powers to his priests, to help him in his apostolic task, but the bond between them remained so close that it was customary to speak of "the priest of such and such a bishop." And priests, deacons, and subdeacons—all the clergy of the city—lived with the bishop in community. The priest Chromatius was thus attached to Bishop Valerian, who had succeeded an Arian, but was himself a Catholic who worked hard with his clergy to destroy Arianism in his diocese. Around him there gradually grew a group of tremendously fervent friends, in the forefront of whom were Jerome and Bonosus, and soon some of their other student friends, including Rufinus and Heliodorus. Together they studied theology, and thrilled over their discovery of the monastic life. The Gospel lived heroically, as it had been at first, was for Jerome a revelation. In these surroundings, at once ardent and learned, he found complete satisfaction both for his studious tastes and his zeal as a new convert—for it was a true conversion that turned him from a moderate Christian to a total Christian. "The clerics of Aquileia are like a choir of the blessed," he wrote. It seemed to him that he had found from the start everything needed for a lifetime: the love of Christ, friendship, and the life of the mind; indeed it was of all these that his life was to be made up, but not in the way he imagined in this happy circle at Aquileia. But while there he did form friendships that were to have the most profound influence upon him. It was at Aquileia that he met the aged Paul, who came, like Rufinus, from Concordia: an amazing scholar, nearly a hundred years old, he had a rich library, and despite his great age, was still able to read, expound, and dispute. Jerome listened as he spoke of his past: he had in his youth known a cleric who had been secretary to St. Cyprian, the famous Bishop of Carthage, whose name took one back more than a century, for his bishopric coincided with the terrible persecution of Decian in 250, and he was martyred eight years later, decapitated at the gates of his own episcopal city.

Some of the guests who passed through were also to leave their mark upon Jerome's life—among others Evagrios, a priest from Antioch, later to become bishop of that city. Through him Jerome received direct knowledge of the life of the eastern monks which so fascinated him.

And, as so often happens, the circle of friends continued to grow; in Chromatius' house, his mother and sisters lived consecrated to God; not far away, at Hemona (now Liubliana), other girls had grouped together—there were no convents as yet—to practice an evangelical way of life. Jerome used to visit them, passing on to them his knowledge, both profane and sacred, and lending them his manuscripts—for he was still indefatigably copying everything he could lay hands on, finding much of value in the library of Paul of Concordia, thanks to whom he made his first contact with the great Christian writers, St. Cyprian himself, Tertullian, St. Hilary of Poitiers.

Yet all this happy devotion was to be brought to a sudden end. At the beginning of the year 374, Jerome left Aquileia, and not only Jerome, but the whole group was dispersed. What exactly happened? It is generally agreed that Jerome had by then quarreled with his parents, but that would not explain the departure of the others; Rufinus, who left for Egypt, Bonosus who became a hermit on an island in the Adriatic, Heliodorus who set out on a pilgrimage to Jerusalem, Evagrios and another companion, Innocentius, who went back to Antioch. From some passages in their letters, it has been deduced that the trouble was caused by Jerome's connection with the virgins at Hemona; Jerome himself alludes to unworthy accusations by his Aunt Castorina. He defended himself violently. Perhaps, quite simply, it required a more pliable character and a less biting tongue than his to escape calumny and do nothing imprudent in a situation where the Arians were ever ready to attack, and there may also have been opposition from that Bishop of Striden whom Jerome compared to the cover of a cooking pot.

"A sudden cyclone carried me far away from you in its force; the close attachment that bound us together was succeeded by the wicked rending that tore us apart," he wrote later to Rufinus. His farewells to his family did nothing to set matters right; two years

35

later he declared that his family had not written to him once. However Stridon, which had never meant much in his life, was shortly to be struck off the map, for in 378 the town was totally destroyed in the invasion of the Goths, who were only with great difficulty driven back; today, indeed, we cannot even be sure exactly where it stood.

The cyclone in question made Jerome determine to fulfill his dream, and join the ascetics of the desert. He set off for Antioch, on foot, as a monk and a pilgrim should. But Jerome was by no means athletic; it seems as though his health was always delicate; the summer heat exhausted him, and the road was long. He has listed for us his "uncertain and wandering ramblings"—Thrace, Pontus, Bithynia, Galatia, Cappadocia, and Cilicia. He more or less followed the old postal route, and indeed the road that the Crusaders were later to take, along the shores of the Adriatic, northern Greece, the Bosphorus, then Asia Minor (now Turkey), and finally northern Syria.

Once in Antioch, he had to stop, utterly worn out. Luckily for him, the house of his friend the priest Evagrios was ready for him. He was a guest there for almost a year, reading and working, but above all, restoring his health. "I am at present rejoicing in my dear Evagrios," he wrote. "He is my one eye, he is everything to me; and I, constantly ill, have attached myself to him as though to make his work harder."

In so weak a state he naturally had little resistance to epidemics, and there seems to have been a really terrible one in Antioch that year. Two of Jerome's best friends were to die of it—Innocentius, and one Hylas who was there, having been sent from Egypt by Antonia Melania, an important woman in Christian society, near whom Rufinus was living. "About the middle of Lent," he writes, "the fever took hold of the center of my being, it invaded my exhausted body, left it no rest, and though it is hard to believe it, my limbs were so eaten up by it that I was held together almost solely by my bones. Indeed, they were preparing for my funeral, for life, breath, warmth—my body was already cold—beat only in the one warm corner of my breast."

It was then that the dream came to him which was so decisive. Whatever may have been the exact circumstances in which it took place, it certainly gave the direction to the rest of Jerome's life; here is his own account of it: "Suddenly my soul was caught up in ecstasy. There was the judge's tribunal; I was dragged toward it, and the light around it was so dazzling that I dared not raise my eyes from the ground where I lay. I was asked what my condition was. 'I am a Christian,' I replied. Then he who sat on the throne replied, 'You lie; you are a Ciceronian, not a Christian; where your treasure is, there also your heart is.'"

He finishes the story, explaining that during his vision he swore to give up his study of pagan literature. There has been much speculation as to what really happened on this occasion. At first Jerome, recounting his experience in the letter I have just quoted, attached great importance to it, but when he returned to the subject much later, he seems to minimize it. What is certain is that at this time he made a decisive choice. He was then twenty-seven; there could be no doubt of his marked bent for literature, but up till now, like all the young men of his age, this was directed solely toward pagan literature which was naturally all that was used at that time for training the minds of the young; he therefore honestly believed that culture could only mean that ancient culture imbued with paganism. And it was a tremendous sacrifice to dedicate himself, as he did, to the study of the Bible—whose riches he was only later to discover. He did not realize the fruitfulness of the country he was opening; he did not know that, along with Augustine, Ambrose, and so many others of his own and later centuries, he was inaugurating a new, Christian culture. It is these and their successors who form the foundations of the magnificent flowering of literature, philosophy, and indeed of all things human, of the Middle Ages, which was to leave Cicero so far behind. As one of their number pointed out, they could see further, even if they were only, as he humbly declared, "dwarfs lifted up on the shoulders of giants." Up till then, antiquity had seemed the only possible prototype for beauty, art, science, and even poetry; yet other springs were to be found which would prove infinitely richer and more fertile.

38

5

The Desert

At last the day came when Jerome took what he believed to be the decisive step: he left Antioch to bury himself in the desert of Chalcis. He had long hesitated, accusing himself of being lacking in courage, begging his friends "to deliver him by their prayers from the darkness of this world. . . . It is for me to wish," he wrote, "but your prayers must win for me the will and the power." His illness, and the deaths of his friends, seem to have given him the willpower he needed. For some time he hoped to take his friend Heliodorus with him, but the latter

39

decided, after some hesitation, to go back to Italy, whither Evagrios also was bound. He was to become bishop of Altinum. Thus it was alone, though encouraged by the example of Bonosus, that he set out for the south in the autumn of 375.

Jerome was then about twenty-eight, and had already two pieces of writing to his credit. One was a short account—a "conte noir," his biographer Jean Steinmann calls it—of an adventure his friend Evagrios had experienced a few years earlier: he had persuaded the emperor to grant a pardon to a woman in Vercelle, who was accused, possibly unjustly, of adultery, and had in some extraordinary way survived the executioner's sword, so that the clerics whose job it was to bury her noticed that she was in fact still alive, and nursed her back to health. His other work, written after the famous dream, prefigured his future career, for it was a work of exegesis, a commentary on one of the Old Testament prophets—Abdias.

He came now to the fringe of the desert, fully determined to give up everything that had made up his past life; this new parting was even more radical than the one he was to recall when he went to Jerusalem: "Home, father and mother, sister, family, and, harder, still, the habit of eating well—all this I gave up for the kingdom of heaven. . . ."

The Syrian desert where he went was provided at the spot he chose—Qinnesrin, south of Aleppo—with natural caves, in which there were a few monks living.

Jerome came to join them with his customary enthusiasm: "O desert, adorned with the flowers of Christ! O solitude which gives birth to the stones celebrated in the Apocalypse that will build the city of the great King! O hermitage where one may enjoy the intimacy of God!"

Before long he came up against the harder realities. He had embraced asceticism joyfully and resolutely; he describes himself as "hideous beneath the scratchy sackcloth he wore," which suggests that he did in fact wear a hair shirt; but he had not foreseen the effects of an overaustere life upon his already delicate health, nor of poor food on his stomach: "My dirty skin looked like the skin of a Negro; always weeping and groaning, when, in spite of myself, sleep overcomes me, my bones, which seem barely joined, almost crack on the bare ground. Of the food and drink I say nothing; even the sick take only cold water—to warm anything would be luxury."

But despite—or perhaps because of—this excessive severity toward himself, he was beset with temptations: "I, who, through fear of hell had sentenced myself to so harsh a prison, with no companions but scorpions and wild beasts, often felt as though I were dancing among girls. Fasting had taken all color from my face, but the soul in my frozen body was inflamed with desires, and, weak as I was, my flesh half dead, the only fire I felt was the fire of lust."

Yet so strong was his will that he resisted these

41

temptations successfully. His strongest weapon, after prayer, was study. So he gave himself to the study of the Bible. But he was at once faced with a difficulty: his critical mind was not slow to find the errors in the Latin translation of the Bible they used at the time; even the Septuagint text—the Greek translation of the Hebrew books made in the third century, upon which the Latin was based—did not satisfy a mind so eager for exactitude. Then an opportunity presented itself to learn Hebrew. There was among the monks a convert Jew, who introduced him to this "barbarous" language. Jerome, from then on, followed the way marked out for him as an exegete and textual critic— despite the difficulties he described to his friends: "My whole soul was aflame with evil thoughts. To defeat them, I placed myself under the guidance of a Jewish convert monk. . . . The words I had to learn were hissing and gasping. Oh! what work! what difficulties I had to conquer; how often did I despair and give up, and then stubbornly resolving to learn, return to my study; my conscience bears witness to the agonies I endured, and inflicted upon those who shared my life. But I thank God for it; the bitter seed of this study has given me the sweetest fruit."

As well as this beginning of Hebrew, Jerome was deepening his knowledge of Greek, and he continued, unwearyingly, to enrich his library by copying manuscripts. He kept writing to his friends to ask for the books he wanted—those of St. Hilary, Tertullian, and

so on. He had round him copyists whom he called
his pupils; it is thought that these may have been
abandoned children found and adopted by the monks;
whoever they were, he dictated texts to them, and was
able to place the fruits of their labors at the disposal
of his friends.

It was while he was at Chalcis that he wrote the
history of St. Paul the Hermit which I have already
spoken of; it was indeed a hard-working retreat; when
he left the desert he was able to say of himself: "I
have taken nothing from anybody; I did not receive
charity like an idler; it was by the sweat of my arm
that I won my daily bread."

It was then also that he began that tremendous
task of letter-writing which ended only with his life.
He wrote to his friends, which to some extent made
up for the moral solitude he often felt. He often
spoke of the joy he got from the letters he received in
answer from those same friends—those in Aquileia,
for instance, who gave him news of his family, among
others of his young sister whom he felt also to be
drawn to the monastic life, and whom on one occasion
he strongly recommended to the Bishop of Aquileia,
Valerian. Of his enormous correspondence, there remain to us only a hundred and fifty-four letters posi-
tively identified, but from time to time others are
found, and as his biographers say, "there is no reason
to think that the era of discoveries is finally closed"
(J. Labourt). Some of these letters, indeed, are verita-

ble treatises, so that they can be classed as dogmatic letters, or exegetical letters, and so forth, according to the subject.

But Jerome was far from finding in the desert that peace, that moral tranquillity which he had gone there to seek. As well as his private temptations, there were controversies with the other monks so violent that, less than three years after arriving there, he had once again to make up his mind to leave.

When Jerome left Antioch, the town had been torn among three religious factions, each with its own bishop. One was Euzios, an Arian; another, Meletius, was suspected of Arianism; the third, Paulinus, was elected by a small group of the unwaveringly orthodox. Paulinus, upheld by Evagrios, also had the support of the Pope. In 374, however, yet another bishop, Vitalis, was acclaimed by some schismatics.

We can imagine the impassioned disputes of their various supporters; the church in Antioch was completely divided by them, and these divsions affected the monks as well. In general, those in the desert of Chalcis supported Meletius, whereas Jerome, a foreigner among them—a westerner among easterners —was a friend of Paulinus. This alone was enough to render him suspect in the eyes of many of them.

The great question that divided them was that of *hypostases*—a term taken sometimes to mean "substance," and sometimes, "divine person." Partisans of one or the other bishop kept coming to urge him to commit himself on this question of hypostases. Jerome did his best to remain neutral amid all these disputes; he protested against them in a letter to the priest Marcus who also sought to put an end to them: "As for me, like a deaf man I hear nothing, like a dumb man I keep my mouth shut," he wrote, paraphrasing Scripture. But it was precisely this refusal to reply, accompanied, no doubt, by the caustic remarks that his nature always led him to make, which exasperated everyone to the point of fury. It seems that the one thing they all finally agreed upon was to brand him a heretic: "I feel I must protest aloud against the barbarism of this land," he cried, again to Marcus . . . "I am called heretic when I preach the consubstantial Trinity; I am accused of Sabellian impiousness when I unwearyingly proclaim three persons, subsistent, real, complete, and perfect; from the Arian standpoint I am indeed heretical, but from the orthodox, those who criticize such a faith are orthodox no longer; let them, then, condemn me as a heretic along with the West and with Egypt, in other words, with Damasus and Peter."

It was the representative of Peter to whom he finally decided to appeal—that is, to Pope Damasus, whom he may have known when he was in Rome. His letter gives a good description of the state of tension existing among the monks of Chalcis: "In the desert, the struggle is greater than ever. On one side is the roaring rage of the Arians, held and upheld by the world"—the Emperors, remember, were more or less on the Arian side—"on the other the three fragments of a divided church are all striving to draw me to them; the traditional authority of the monks round about stands against me . . . Meletius, Vitalis, and Paulinus all claim to adhere to you. If only one made this claim I might believe him; but as it is, either two of them, or all three, are lying." We do not know what was Damasus' reply to this letter, nor to a second in a similar tone. But the day finally came when Jerome could no longer bear the attitude of these monks, and determined to leave Chalcis: "I am ashamed to say," he wrote, summing up the situation, "that from the caves of our cells we condemn the universe; in our sackcloth and ashes, we pass judgment upon bishops; what is the Emperor's soul doing beneath his pentitential garb? . . . Better to live among wild beasts than among such Christians. . . ."

6

Constantinople and Rome

In the spring of 378, Jerome came back to Antioch. It was then that his friend Bishop Paulinus ordained him priest, but without obliging him to exercise any priestly functions. Otherwise he did not stay long in the city, though he did have occasion to hear one of the best (though not the most orthodox) exegetes of the time, Apollinarius of Laodicea. Exegesis was clearly attracting him more and more, and it was undoubtedly to deepen his knowledge of the Bible that he set off next for Constantinople, the capital of the Eastern Empire.

There he was taught by the man he was always to consider supremely his master, St. Gregory of Nazianzen. Gregory had just been named Bishop of Constantinople amid circumstances of turmoil. Up till then, given the position of the Emperor Valens, this see had been filled only by Arians. But in 378 Valens was killed at Adrianople while fighting the Goths and the Huns. Gratian, who succeeded him, handed over the Eastern Empire the following year to a Spanish general, Theodosius, who was orthodox. His first thought was to promulgate an edict in 380 restoring the orthodox faith to its rights, and it was under his aegis that Gregory was invited to fill the see of Constantinople. The church of Sancta Sophia remained for some time in Arian hands, and disputes with the Arians were to continue till the Council of 381.

Gregory of Nazianzen had been a rhetor; then, like Jerome, he was drawn to the monastic life; like him, too, he was sensitive and delicate, and his eloquence sometimes drew applause from its hearers; he was also a fine poet, with a mind both deep and clear. In other words, he had a lot in common with Jerome, who listened to his sermons, particularly on the Trinity, and was profoundly affected by them. His stay in Constantinople brought a wealth of new knowledge and new friendship, for there too he made the acquaintance of Gregory of Nyssa. This latter, whose works became an authority in themselves, was the brother of St. Basil the Great, Basil of Caesarea, who died in 379, and who produced the famous "Rule" still observed today by the monks in the east. We can see, then, how familiar were the preoccupations he found there; he also mentions the Treatise on theology (no longer in existence), which St. Amphilocus, Bishop of Iconium, wrote and gave him, concerning the Holy Ghost. From all this we get some idea of the atmosphere of the time in these Christian circles, thrilled as they were by their ever-deepening discovery of their own faith, and gradually building the foundations of the theology that was to nourish the world of the future.

It was in this atmosphere that Jerome composed his first great work of scholarship. It was, in part, a translation of the Chronicon of Eusebius of Caesarea. Evidently his first introduction to exegesis had made him feel the need of a sound chronological basis. Eusebius' work gave him one, and he wanted to make its help available to the Western world by translating it into Latin. This Chronicon, or Chronicle of Eusebius was a kind of summary of the history of the world; though full of errors, it is still one of the works on which our knowledge of the ancient world rests. As edited by Jerome, the work was in three parts: the first, from Abraham to the Trojan War, was simply a translation of Eusebius' text; the second, from the Trojan War to the twentieth year of Constantine's reign (325), contained, as well as Eusebius' work, some additions by Jerome himself (especially in regard to Roman history, in which Eusebius, being a Greek, was not sufficiently interested). And finally, he set about adding a third part which was to cover the time from 325 until the present—the death of Valens in 378; in it he noted the chief political events, and also religious matters, and the names of authors, sacred and profane. Jerome being Jerome, though ever a careful and scrupulous historian, there is still a personal note to be found, for instance, in his mention of certain "outstanding" monks—his own friends Bonosus, Rufinus, and Florentinus.

This translation, though much criticized when it first appeared, was to be tremendously successful in later times. The immense attention paid to the study of history throughout the Middle Ages bears witness to its importance in the eyes of the Church, embedded and incarnate as she is in time. Jerome's work formed a splendid foundation for that historical knowledge, and, as he wrote, his detractors had an easy enough time: "only those who never write are never criticized." A preoccupation with history was always to remain in the forefront of Jerome's mind. He toyed with the idea of writing a history of his time, but, unhappily for us, this was never realized. When one thinks what a fertile age it was for the Church, and, with all its turmoil, how rich in literature and thought, one cannot but regret his not having done so. To complete his work, he longed for a respite from the Barbarian invasions which made the Empire look so unstable and the future so uncertain—an impression which did not, as we shall see, belie the facts.

But he did not lose his concern for exegesis. Thus —also during his stay in Constantinople—we find him translating twenty-eight homilies of Origen, some on Jeremias, some on Ezechiel. He thus enriched the West with the work of that famous apologist, who had restored the Alexandrian school, and done so much to make the Church illustrious in the first half of the third century. He flung himself enthusiastically into the study of these scriptural works, which followed the so-called "allegorical" method, whereby the commentator interpreted each passage in the sacred books, developing all the hidden images in each. This method could lead to excesses, as when Origen, writing of the vision of Isaias, says that the two seraphim in the temple on either side of the throne of God mean Christ and the Holy Ghost. When Jerome himself came to comment on the same passage, he refused any such dubious interpretation, and saw the two as an image of the Old and New Testaments, with Christ occupying the throne.

For, like Origen, Jerome turned from translating to writing his own books. And he developed the science of exegesis in his turn, not merely content as Origen had been, with explaining the symbolism, but introducing what we now call criticism of the texts themselves. It was becoming more and more clear that he was a really great scholar who felt the need of basing his study of the Bible on known facts—with authentic texts, accurate translations, and exact chronology.

In the midst of all this work came the Council of Constantinople.

This council took place in the spring of 381; it considered a great many ideas and a great many holders of ideas, but most powerful attacks of the Arians failed. Orthodoxy triumphed; heresies were condemned, and St. Gregory of Nazianzen was officially enthroned in Sancta Sophia. However, it still remained to decide the question of the see of Antioch. One of the claimants, Meletius, died during the council. Some, among them Gregory, proposed to fix upon Paulinus, Jerome's friend; but he had enemies, and the dispute went on and on until at last Gregory decided to resign from the see of Constantinople; a Cilician, Nectarius, was chosen in his place, and in Antioch, they chose Flavian. Thus defeated, Paulinus resolved to go to Rome, where another council was being convoked through the efforts of the western Emperor, Gratian. Jerome decided to go with him.

He had not been back to Rome since his youth, since the period of his studies and his baptism. The fifteen years that had passed since then had been important ones for him, and during them he had acquired something of a reputation, as well as making a certain number of enemies, as so strong a personality

must. It is not surprising, then, that Pope Damasus'
attention was drawn to him.

Damasus himself was a surprising figure. He had
been made Pope in rather dramatic circumstances.
When his predecessor, Pope Liberius, died in 366,
the clergy of Rome were divided; two gatherings took
place, and the more important of them, in the basilica
of St. Laurence in Lucina, elected the deacon Damasus; the other, in Santa Maria in Trastevere, chose
the deacon Ursinus. The supporters of the two sides
attacked each other, and actually came to blows—
indeed there were even some deaths. The prefect of
Rome intervened and Ursinus was exiled. But his
supporters would not admit defeat, and continued to
hold their basilica. And when Damasus' supporters
made their final attack, there was once again fighting
and bloodshed. After a year of exile, Ursinus returned
to Rome, and trouble started again. Obviously such
internecine warfare did nothing to improve the prestige of the Church.

Yet it was in his pontificate that some of the
most decisive progress was made. One element of
this was purely negative: in 382, the Emperor Gratian
decided to let paganism die a natural death. He
stopped making allowance for worship, whereby the
state had, up till then, paid the expenses of the sacri-
fices, of the upkeep of the temples, the soothsayers, and
the vestal virgins. This step was not taken without
protests, however; one of the leading objectors was a

highly placed pagan functionary called Symmachus. It was he who, in 385, was to offer a job as professor of rhetoric in Milan to a brilliant young North African, a certain Aurelius Augustine—who was to take his advice, quite without any idea that there he would have the most decisive encounter of his life, with the bishop of that city (a relative of Symmachus'), Ambrose.

It was an inspiring age that witnessed the crossing of the paths of Jerome, Ambrose, and Augustine on the streets of Rome.

Each, however, was to follow a very different path thenceforth. One of the greatest days in Jerome's life was the one on which he received this letter:

"I have read the commentaries in Greek and Latin on the interpretation of the gospels which our people, I mean those who are orthodox, have written, both in the past, and recently, on the text: Hosanna to the Son of David. Their ideas are not merely different, but contradictory. Your love is known for its warmth and boldness. Write me honestly what is the sense of the Hebrew, eliminating all conjecture, and dispelling doubt. Thus, in this matter as in so many others, our solicitude will obtain grace for you in Christ Jesus." The letter was signed, "Damasus, Bishop."

No one could have been more appreciative of Jerome's personality than Damasus. As a former archivist of the Church in Rome he had been concerned to ascertain the major facts about the underground life of the first Christian centuries at a moment when a new page in the Church's history was clearly opening; he thus possessed both a sense of the past, and a strong awareness of the needs of his own age. It is to Damasus that we owe the inscriptions made in the fourth century to perpetuate the memory of the martyrs—St. Agnes, among others. In the catacombs he found out which tombs were which, and composed epitaphs for the saints based on their "passions," those stories of their martyrdoms which were handed down by word of mouth. For the carving of his inscriptions, he even used for the first time a new style of lettering, created by an artist, Furius Dionysius Filocalus, and known therefore as Filocalian characters. This is but one instance of the complete renewal Christianity was bringing even into the artistic field, of that ardent inventiveness the Church was to show in being always in the forefront of the artistic movement right up to the end of the fifteenth century.

Damasus, historian, archeologist, and poet, was not slow to see in Jerome the man to help him in his work; he chose him to be his secretary, and there was to be henceforth a kind of affectionate competition between the old bishop and the young scholar: "You are asleep; for a long time you have been reading more than you have been writing! Here are a few questions I have decided to send you to wake you up," wrote Damasus to Jerome. . . .

"Yesterday, for example, the despatch you sent me

contained no letters other than those you dictated long ago in the desert, which I have already devoured and copied, and since you spontaneously promised to take time at night to dictate whatever work I might ask, I accept with enthusiasm what I should certainly have demanded in any case, had you failed to offer it. I do not believe that our discussions can have any more worthy subject than the Scriptures: we shall talk, I questioning, you answering. Nothing in the world could please me more. . . ."

From this letter we can easily imagine the relationship between the Pope and his secretary. The former questioning, spurring on the zeal of the other—who needed no spur, for up to the very end of his life, his most marked trait was his enthusiasm; he always loved research, and never flagged in his ardent wish to discover the truth underlying every approximation. We can follow the thread of their conversations; for example, when Damasus asked Jerome for a commentary on the parable of the prodigal son, or set before him the difficulties he had found in Genesis, upon which he wanted the exegete's advice.

As for Jerome, one gets the impression that with such encouragement and understanding he was perfectly happy. He worked with more unwearying enthusiasm than ever, continuing to improve his Hebrew, and even getting the Jews in Rome to lend him books from their synagogue of which he rapidly made copies. And all the time, he never stopped complaining of his difficulties, of how his eyes were hurting, or that his copyists were unsatisfactory, and so on.

". . . Yesterday you sent me word that you wanted a letter; I think this is more in the nature of notes, short replies to questions, each of which would require whole volumes in answer. . . . I await your orders: am I to reduce the explanation you want into the space of one letter, or am I to write a volume on each point? . . . If so, then you will think I am only sleeping, since for you to read without writing is to sleep. Forgive my delayed and hastily written reply; the haste is because I dictate in an evening what should really take days; the delay is because I was too busy to answer your questions at once."

It was a sheer intuition of genius, or rather, perhaps, an inspiration of the Holy Ghost, that made Pope Damasus set Jerome's feet on the road of his life's work, the translation into Latin of the Scriptures. Up till then, as we have seen, the many Latin versions were most inadequate. Jerome had what was required to make the really accurate translation the time called for; his knowledge of Greek and Hebrew, his tremendous scholarship, and also—very important—his profound sense of poetry and his great fervor, all fitted him for this huge undertaking. In his ardor, he did even more than the Pope had asked of him, for having begun by retranslating the gospels, he ended by making a new translation of the entire Bible.

His method in establishing the text he was to

work on was the same as that used by scholars in our own day. A good translation must first involve the establishment of a correct text. There were often mistakes in the manuscripts; so his first work must be to compare them, to try and discover which version was correct on the points on which they differed— in other words, what we would today call textual criticism. Jerome describes it in his preliminary letter to Pope Damasus: "I must bring together the copies of Scripture scattered round the world. As they differ among themselves, I must first decide which agree best with the original Greek." His scholarship has not been found wanting here, for the recension he chose was the same as the famous *Codex Sinaiticus,* whose excellence is recognized by scholars today.

After the gospels, he turned next to revising the Psalter. This work, like the first, was to receive more criticism than praise; it upset habits, it corrected mistakes that were part of everyone's routine, and anything that does this must always arouse protests. He had no illusions about the fact: "Whoever comes, whether lettered or ignorant, and picks up this volume —as soon as he realizes what he is reading, will, before even drawing breath, cry that I am sacrilegious and a forger. That I should have dared to add, modify, or correct these ancient books in any way at all! . . . Two things console me for this: the fact that you, the Sovereign Pontiff, have commanded me, and the fact that, as even my enemies must agree, not

all the former versions can be correct. They say one
must rely on the Latin text—but which Latin text?
There are as many texts as there are manuscripts. If
all one can do is decide on a middle path of truth
among them, why not return to the Greek sources?"

While working at this, he also undertook to translate Origen's homilies on the Canticle of Canticles,
and himself composed a polemical work, the Treatise
against Helvidius. The said Helvidius was an Arian
who had written a work in which he denied the
virginity of Mary, at least after Christ's birth, and
attacked the whole Christian idea of virginity. In his
reply, Jerome made use of all the resources of exegesis
at his disposal; in particular he found no difficulty
in showing that the phrase "brethren of Jesus," which
Helvidius had insisted on interpreting literally, can
only have meant Our Lord's first cousins. Jerome also
produced a magnificent eulogy of Christian virginity,
which was to influence many in times to come. It is
hard for us now to realize what a stumbling block
virginity was in the society that gave birth to Christianity. All Jewish custom went to exalt maternity
above everything; whereas the pagans allowed woman
no legal rights as a person at all; she was a perpetual
minor, passing from the control of her father to that
of her husband. To remain celibate was to set oneself
against the power of the paterfamilias, who could do
what he chose with his daughters. The very idea of
equality between men and women was still, in

Jerome's day, thought of as monstrous, at least in pagan society.

Thus the Church found itself in total opposition to the Greco-Roman world when, from the first, not only did it proclaim that men and women were equal, but also put forward as an ideal that virginity should be preserved for love of God. Yet, encouraged by the counsels of St. Paul, from apostolic times onward, there had been virgins who gloriously practiced the evangelical counsels, and following Our Lady and St. John, observed perfect chastity (He that heareth, let him understand.) The Church gave a special honor to those young virgins, most of whom were martyred—Agnes, Agatha, Cecilia.

Jerome adopted his normal, fiery tone in his reply to Helvidius, but he adds to it a personal note, a kind of apologia:

"I presume that, having been defeated by the truth, you will now calumniate my life and revenge yourself by defaming me. . . . I must inform you that your insults will honor me, for the mouth you use to slander me has been used to outrage Mary, and the baying of your words will unite the servant of the Lord with His Mother."

Indeed Jerome, during this stay in Rome, took a most active part in the monastic movement that was beginning. Faithful to his own ascetic ideal, he encouraged some Roman society women to take the same path, and his name became inseparably linked with theirs.

It was one of their number, Marcella, who supplied the impetus to form a little group of virgins and widows who gathered together in her splendid villa on the Aventine. Among those who came was a rich widow, Paula, still young—she was barely thirty—who had a young son Toxotius, and four daughters, Blesilla, Eustochium, Ruffina, and Paulina. Paulina was to marry a former companion of Jerome's, now a senator, Pammachius. The other three were drawn to the ascetic ideal to which several of their friends had already vowed themselves, women whose names we are later to find among Jerome's group—Lea, Asella, Fabiola, and others.

With such a master to lead them, these young Roman society women were not slow in developing both their spirit of charity and their religious education. For Jerome, not content to let them merely carry out devotional practices, set to work to develop their faith, by leading them to draw from his own wellspring of sacred texts, and determined to interest them in the study of Hebrew which had proved so fruitful for himself. Paula was to end by being able to sing the psalms in Hebrew. All gave evidence of an intellectual ardor hard to envisage in women who had once been so worldly. Jerome's course of studies was no longer enough for them; his letters show what questions they would bombard him with between one instruction and the next; to Marcella, for instance, he writes:

"The task of a letter is to give news in writing of the family and one's day-to-day life. . . . But you, completely absorbed and preoccupied with learned books, write me nothing that does not rack my brains and force me to examine Scripture. Yesterday, having set me a tremendous problem, you asked what I thought about it, and demanded that I reply to you at once in writing. You began the letter with the question . . . 'What is the "linen ephod" with which the prophet Samuel girded himself? Is it a belt? or, as some think, a censer, or rather some kind of garment?' . . . You then pass on to the Book of Judges . . .: 'What is "teraphim"?' "

Evidently the students of Jerome's school were not content with generalities, but passed every text they studied through a fine sieve of criticism. Thus, under his aegis, a real school of perfection and religious knowledge was taking shape among these Roman noblewomen. For Eustochium, Jerome composed what amounted to a treatise on virginity which was to form the earliest Rule of these cloisterless nuns. His letter to her was cherished down the ages; even in the Middle Ages, it was translated into French thirteenth century verse.

Then one of Paula's daughters, Blesilla, died. She had been married, and widowed within seven months, after which she turned from a fairly worldly life to

follow the same ascetic ideal as her mother and sisters.
At the age of twenty, an illness carried her off in a
few days; Paula was so griefstricken that she fainted
at the funeral. The letter Jerome wrote her on this
occasion is most moving; in it he speaks of Blesilla's
young face, changing so quickly from the vanity usual
in one of her age and position to an impassioned ardor
for study and the search for perfection. And he
promises her mother that he will make Blesilla live
in human memory through his own works: "I swear
it, I promise, it is she who will sing my words, it is
to her that my labors will be dedicated. . . . Her
memory, lasting forever, will make up for the short-
ness of her life. She lives in heaven with Christ, and
she will live also in the mouths of men. . . . Thanks
to my books she will never die."

Only a month after Blesilla, Pope Damasus died,
on December 11, 384. For Jerome there now began a
time of great difficulties; calumny and direct attack
on him personally came thick and fast, and forced him
once again to take his departure.

Such attacks were not new. Jerome had all the
various sects against him—Montanists, Arians, supporters of Novation, all were so many enemies to him;
but for all his zeal in fighting for orthodoxy, he had
not drawn to himself the sympathy of all the orthodox.
There were all those who hated his "innovations"
in the text of Scripture; there were those others who
felt just as strongly about his strong views on marriage

and virginity—and here the epistle to Eustochium caused much scandal. Then, too, more than one had been the object of Jerome's sharp and mocking tongue, which spared no one. There were at this time a great many worldly prelates in Rome, living well cushioned lives; Jerome's asceticism was a living reproach to them, and they could hardly fail to see themselves in portraits such as this:

"There are some who aspire to the priesthood and the diaconate simply to have more freedom in seeing women; all that concerns these men are their clothes, their perfumes, that they do not dance in ill-fitting shoes; their waving hair has been shaped by the curling iron, their fingers sparkle with rings, and lest the damp footpath wet their feet, they go on the tips of their toes; they look more like young lovers than clerics. There are some who spend all their time and effort on learning the names of married women, their addresses, and their habits. . . ." He goes on to picture the prelate who is greedy, a flatterer, avaricious, womanizing, and so on.

As long as Damasus lived, his secretary was unassailable. Some six months after his death, Jerome was summoned to appear before an ecclesiastical court. He had no trouble in clearing himself of the accusations brought against him, but he was ordered to return to the church of Antioch to which he belonged. He did so. As he was about to embark at Ostia with his brother Paulinian he sent a letter to

Asella, a woman in Roman society, in which he poured out his rancor against his attackers:

"Before I became familiar with the house of holy Paula, the whole city agreed in thinking highly of me; I was thought worthy by nearly everyone of the papacy; it was said that Damasus, of happy memory, had my very words on his lips; I was called a saint, I was called humble, and learned. . . . O envy, which is the first to destroy itself, O deceit of Satan, which will always persecute goodness. . . . If it were pagans or Jews who attacked this way of life, I would be gladly consoled by being hated by those who hated Christ. . . . But what anguish have I suffered, I who have fought for the cross. False and infamous accusations have been made, but," he concludes, "I know that one comes to the Kingdom of Heaven without reference to one's good or bad reputation."

7

Bethlehem

When he left Rome, Jerome was convinced he would never see it again; at thirty-eight, he was beginning a new period in his life, which was to be both the most stable and the most fruitful.

Jerome's departure led to another: Paula with her daughter Eustochium, and some of the other Roman virgins who had been his pupils. All were determined to continue their way of perfection and their biblical studies under the guidance of their spiritual master. Before settling down, they set out with him upon a pilgrimage, as a prelude to the spiritual journey they had set themselves for the future. All together they thus followed the path taken by those innumerable pilgrims who were to journey to Jerusalem in the Middle Ages, sometimes braving the most appalling dangers, particularly after the Moslem conquest—the same to be taken by those pilgrims in arms who fought the first Crusade.

Jerome gives an account of this pilgrimage in the Epitaph of Paula. He tells how, after staying near St. Epiphanus in Cyprus, then in Antioch, where the pilgrims seem to have come together, "the noble woman who used to be carried in a litter by eunuchs, set off in the saddle on the back of a small donkey." One can imagine what such a journey must have meant with such a guide as Jerome, conversant with every smallest detail of the history of each place. They first followed Elias' path along the banks of Sarepta, then the beaches of Tyre "where Paul had prayed on his knees," and Acre which was, eight centuries later, to become the fortified bastion of Christendom. They then came to a halt in Caesarea where there were many memories of the past—the home of Cornelius the centurion as well as of Eusebius of Caesarea, but chiefly the place where Origen had lived and collected the material for one of his works, the *Hexapla,* a collection of Bible texts dear to Jerome's heart. Then came Emmaüs, and the holy city, Jerusalem, itself. "The proconsul of Palestine, who knew Paula's family very well, had sent his officials and had the

67

pretorium made ready. But she preferred a humble cell"; and the story goes on to show us Paula hastening to make that pilgrimage to all those holy places in the city which in later devotion became the Way of the Cross.

Then the travelers went to venerate Our Lord's cave in Bethlehem, and it seems that they went on to make various excursions to Judea and even to the Dead Sea. They must have been received in Jerusalem by Jerome's friend Rufinus and another important woman, Melania the Elder, who had been settled there for some years. They continued their pilgrimage by visiting Bethany, where they thought of Lazarus, Martha and Mary, Jericho, and the Jordan. Then, crossing Samaria, they came to Nazareth, and the other holy places in Galilee—Cana, Capharnaum, the Lake of Tiberias and Mount Tabor.

The travelers then decided to go to Egypt. They visited the monasteries of Nitria, where dwelt the monks who had influenced Jerome so strongly, and whose example Paula and Eustochium were proposing to follow.

Meanwhile, Jerome went on to Alexandria to consult one of the greatest exegetes, a pupil of Origen, Didymus the blind. He must have been a curious character, using his memory as a substitute for his sight. Jerome was later to translate his work, *De Spiritu Sancto,* and use it for ammunition against St. Ambrose whom he accused of having plagiarized it.

The pilgrimage was, however, near its end; Paula, who was not strong, could not bear the heat of the Egyptian summer, and they all embarked at Pelusa to return to Palestine.

Bethlehem was where they decided to settle. Jerome explains in a letter to St. Paulinus of Nola why he chose Bethlehem, a quiet out-of-the-way spot, rather than Jerusalem, where the noise and crowds would not suit a monastic foundation:

"Here we find a modest supply of healthy food: bread and milk, vegetables which we grow ourselves, and all the fruits of the countryside. Thus we do not fall asleep at prayer, and our work is not impeded by overeating. In summer the trees give us their shade; in autumn the air is fresh, and the dead leaves give us a peaceful place of rest. In spring, the fields are covered with flowers, and amid the songs of birds, our songs rise sweeter even than theirs.

"When the cold and snow of winter come, we have coal; whether waking or sleeping, I am warm enough. Let the Romans keep their milling crowds; let the arena go on being cruel and the circus noisy; and—for it would be unpardonable to forget our friends—let the ladies' senate continue to organize their salons. For ourselves, our happiness is to adhere to the Lord, and put our trust in him."

Paula had two monasteries built at her own expense, one for Jerome and his companions, and the other for the women. "For three years she lived in very cramped conditions, for that was the time it took to build cells and monasteries," says Jerome, "and then to build near the road a refuge for pilgrims, since Mary and Joseph found no room there." This lovely thought of building an inn for travelers at the place where Christ's mother failed to find one is another thing we find often in medieval piety; along the pilgrimage routes that dominated geography up to the end of the thirteenth century, the number of hospices, hospitals, and shelters for pilgrims was quite fantastic; to be convinced of this, one has only to glance at the map drawn up by the Museum of French Monuments, which shows both the refuges for pilgrims and the churches that were built along the routes to St. James of Compostella; and in Jerusalem itself, it was a hospitaller foundation, the Hospital of St. John, begun before the first crusade, around 1080, which was the origin of the powerful order, at once military and hospitaller, that was to become the Knights of Malta.

Thus Bethlehem, with its smiling countryside seeming almost like a corner of Galilee imported into bleak Judea, was the scene of the first western-built monasteries, which were a realization of that east-west synthesis that was to develop under the aegis of Christianity. It was a tremendous advance, and in later times, indeed throughout the Middle Ages, pilgrims to the spot were to link the memory of St. Jerome and his companions with that of Christ's birth.

70

Modern archaeologists have identified a room partly hollowed out of the rock and now fitted up as an oratory in the Franciscan monastery as the place where St. Jerome lived. Earlier on, it was the site of the house where the canons who looked after the Church of the Nativity lived; Paula's monastery is generally thought to have been south of the basilica, where an Orthodox Greek monastery now stands. Paula had built it with a high tower which could be a place of refuge in time of war. This was no empty precaution at a time when barbarian invasion threatened from every side. But it was all very costly; Paula poured her entire fortune into it, and Jerome was obliged to send his young brother Paulinian to sell what remained of their family property in the neighborhood of devastated Stridon.

We know something of the rule of life adopted by the women through the Epitaph of St. Paula; when Eustochium was their superior (after 404), there were fifty of them: "After Paula had founded the monastery of men, whose direction she had handed over to men, she divided the many virgins who had come together from different places and from all stations in life, high, middle, and low, into three sections or monasteries; they worked and ate separately, but came together for psalmody and prayer. After the singing of the 'Alleluia' which called them together, they were permitted no more rest. . . . In the morning at tierce, sext, none, in the evening,

71

and in the middle of the night, they sang the psalter through in order; none of the sisters could fail to know the psalms, none was dispensed from listening to a passage from the Scriptures every day. Only on Sunday did they go the church next to their dwelling. . . . Thence they returned together to carry on their work, making clothes for themselves or others. . . . All dressed the same; the only linen they used was for drying their hands." And Jerome expatiates on the mortifications Paula imposed on herself, which her nuns must surely have copied: she used no mattress, sleeping simply on the ground, she fasted regularly, and used no seasoning on her food except for a little oil; but he also tells us that those who were sick were well fed, and even had meat. Jerome tells us one amusing story: one day, when Paula was ill, Jerome asked St. Epiphanius, whom he thought might have more influence with her than he, to persuade her to take some wine; but at the end of the interview, it was she who had persuaded Epiphanius never to take wine again himself. Jerome adds: "I tell this story, not because I approve of anyone taking on excessive burdens without due thought of what might be beyond their strength . . ., but because it will show the fervor of her heart."

Jerome's advice to his spiritual daughters was, perhaps surprisingly, marked throughout by its gentleness. He showed himself as a truly considerate father as well as a prudent one, and was always ready to

temper severity with the beauty of poetry: "Be the
cicada of the night. . . . Keep watch like the sparrow
of the desert. . . . Your homeland is heaven. . . .
Do not give ear to evil conversations. . . . When you
give alms, let only God see you. When you fast,
look happy, and do not let your clothes be extraordinary or dirty. . . . Do not try to look too pious, nor
more self-effacing than you need. . . . If you fast
for two days, do not think yourself better than some-
one who does not fast: you fast, but you may get
bad-tempered; that person eats, but perhaps practices
gentleness. . . . Get up two or three times each night
to recite the texts of Scripture that we know by
heart. . . . If you have servants to help you in your
ascetic life, do not be haughty toward them, nor
proud because you are their mistress; you all belong
to the same Spouse. . . . Read much, and study as
much as possible; let sleep always catch you with a
book in your hand; let your nodding head fall on a
holy page. . . . Nothing is hard for those who have
love; no effort is too difficult when you really want
something."

A large part of their daily timetable was devoted
to that study of Holy Scripture which had been
what first drew these virgins to their spiritual master.
He felt that there could be no food for a life of
virtue and prayer to equal the assimilating of the
sacred texts: "Love Holy Scripture and Wisdom will

love you; let your tongue know only Christ, and it will be able only to say what is holy."

We can fill in this outline by noting what Jerome had to say more specifically about monks in his letter to Rusticus, a young Gaul, who asked advice about his vocation. We learn that the monks' occupations allowed for manual work—basket-making, gardening, beekeeping, making fishing nets, but above all, of course, calligraphy—that art to which innumerable monks were later to devote themselves in the medieval monasteries, to which we owe our knowledge of the works of Christian, and even Pagan antiquity, each product of which is a masterpiece, both by the perfection and arrangement of the script, and by the illuminations accompanying it. He also presents the young man with this picture of the monastic life: "You must not give yourself up to your own whims, but live in a monastery under the direction of a single father, in company with several brothers, that you may learn from one humility, and from another patience; from one silence, and from another meekness; you will not do what you want, you will eat what is given to you, and no more than your allotted amount; you will be given your clothing; you will work at your appointed task; you will obey when you do not want to; you will go to bed worn out, and fall asleep on your feet; you will have to get up still drowsy; you will sing psalms by your bed. . . . You will serve your brethren, and wash the feet of others. . . ." And he concludes, "It is hard, tremendous, difficult, but the reward is great." Elsewhere he gives the secret of the joy in this mortified life: "Christ is our all; whoever has given up everything for Christ's sake will find Him alone in exchange for all else, and can boldly cry, 'My inheritance is the Lord!' "

Not that everything went smoothly in the life of these monasteries; as in every other period, scandals occurred, and there was cockle mixed in with the wheat. One letter, though its historicity has been doubted, may well be an allusion to a real event: it exhorts a certain deacon, Sabinian, to penance; he, having seduced a married woman in Italy, had taken refuge in Bethlehem, bearing a letter of recommendation from his bishop, to escape her husband's revenge. There he managed to seduce one of the nuns, and was planning to abscond with her, when their plan was discovered. Jerome's exhortation shows that he did not despair of bringing back the sheep that was lost.

From his writings, it is also clear that Jerome was not only a director of souls, but an excellent educator. He set out a whole program of instruction, first for Paula, daughter of Toxotius and granddaughter of St. Paula, then for a little girl, Pacatula. In both cases the program is entirely based on the Bible. "Let her recite for you each day a certain number of lessons from Scripture, that she may learn the rhythm of the Greek; then let her immediately learn the

Latin." Manual work also has its place as a means of education: "Let her also learn to spin wool, to use a distaff, to hold the spindle bowl steady on her knees, to turn a spindle, to guide the threads with her thumb." But he also allows for games, for dolls which should be attractive, for flowers, and even for cakes and sweets; indeed Jerome was a pioneer in what we nowadays call "active methods," as we can see from this passage: "Make letters for her, either of boxwood or ivory, and tell her their names; she can play with them, and in this way even her playing will teach her . . ., reward her for making syllables, and lure her on with the little presents that give such pleasure at her age." And what admirable wisdom we find in the following:

"Let her study with others whom she can want to imitate, and whose praise will spur her on. You must not scold her if she is slow, but stimulate her mind with compliments; let her find happiness in success, and sorrow in failure. Take care above all that she does not come to dislike studying, for bitterness felt in childhood could well outlast the time of apprenticeship."

And we may add to this the advice which shows his horror of any kind of affectation or snobbery: "See that no feminine affectations of elegance lead your daughter to mangle her words."

8

Last Years

Any attempt to sum up the work of
St. Jerome makes one realize that it was so vast that
even a mere listing would go on long enough to
become boring. His time in Bethlehem, the second
period of his life—almost as long, indeed, as the first,
and far more tranquil—saw the accomplishment of
the tremendous work of revising the Bible, as well as
Commentaries composed on most of the books of the
Old Testament and the New (the best known being
perhaps those on Jonas and the Prophets and St.
Matthew). It is true that, as his mastery of Hebrew

grew more complete, he performed what seem near-miracles: the translation of Judith was made in one night—"the time it took her to destroy Holofernes," as a modern critic, P. Antin, notes. This vast labor gave us the Vulgate, the Biblical text used by the Church to this day, and declared authentic by the Council of Trent. It seems curious that so learned a scholar, working always in the most difficult and inaccessible studies, should have produced the best-seller of all time!

Nor did he stop translating from Greek, and also from Coptic, those authors he thought important for the Church. We may also remember the two essays on the monastic life which he also wrote at this time, the Life of Malchus and the Life of Hilarion. The first is more in the nature of a novel: Malchus is a monk living in the desert—a desert reminiscent of that of Chalcis; his ascetic life is rudely cut short by an invasion of the country by Saracens; Malchus is sold as a slave, and his master forces him to marry another slave, a young Saracen girl; he then finds that she is secretly a Christian. One day Malchus persuades his wife to flee with him; they hide in the deserts, pursued by their master, concealing themselves in caves, fording rivers, in constant danger of being found, until suddenly a lion appears and eats their pursuer. After which Malchus and his wife each found a monastery. The work is, to some extent, autobiographical: it bears traces of the desert paths of Egypt and Syria which Jerome followed with Paula and Eustochium. And the foundations made by Malchus and his wife are recognizably similar in spirit to those of Bethlehem.

The other story is the life of Hilarion, and this is more biographical. Hilarion was thought of by the monks of Palestine as the founder of eremitical life in that country. He was converted and decided to embrace the monastic life while studying in Alexandria; having gone to Anthony in the desert to train under him, he returned to Egypt, not far from Gaza, where he made himself a hut in a deserted spot surrounded by swampland—but it did not remain deserted, for many came to join him. The sick and the possessed were brought to him in great numbers to be healed, and in the end he had to flee from a retreat where he could find no peace, and where, to add to his troubles, he was pursued by the Arian persecutions. He died in Cyprus and was buried there, but one of his disciples stole his body to bring back to Palestine. Throughout his life, Hilarion had been a victim of demonic visions, which Jerome describes in the darkest terms; and his story is scattered with anecdotes which he embroiders on with all his instinct for fiction. There was one story of a charioteer in the circus at Gaza whose rival—a pagan—had put a spell on his horses, but who won the race in spite of this fact, because of Hilarion's blessing. Another tells how this same Hilarion cured a mad camel, another how he led a boa-constrictor which had the people mesmerized with fear to a fire upon which it agreeably allowed itself to be burned. There is yet another story of two monks, one avaricious, the other generous; the first was quite willing to receive Hilarion's friends, but secretly made certain that his wine was guarded, and that no one took his grapes; whereas the generous monk actually offered them the grapes from his; when harvest time came, the generous one found his crop was three times bigger than usual, whereas the other's wine turned at once to vinegar.

Jerome clearly delights in these stories that give his talents as narrator such play; but the interest of these works does not lie solely in them: both the amusing anecdotes, and the terrifying visions help to make the monastic life of the day come alive to us. Jerome, as we have seen, was a poet; he knew that it was not enough to devote oneself to intellectual demonstrations, to treatises that argue to convince; all that really exists for man is what he can love, what has human warmth and life. And these two works have probably done more to foster the monastic ideal than the most eloquent sermons.

One of the most important works of that period is the *De Viris Illustribus*. This was written in the style of Suetonius who produced a book under the same title which was about a series of writers of antiquity. Jerome's was, however, setting out a kind of biographical catalogue of Christian writers. He gave us what was in fact the first Manual of Christian

Literature, with a hundred and thirty entries; the early ones are taken from Eusebius of Caesarea, but those relating to the fourth century which was so rich in Christian literature and thought were original and are quite invaluable. I cannot do better than quote what F. Cavallera, a biographer of Jerome, has to say about it: "It is the birth of the literary history of Christianity, and a kind of declaration of the existence of a Christian literature as distinct from profane literature, comparable with it in form, but far superior to it in content." In the Middle Ages this literature was to go even further, for it was to break with the older literature even in its forms, and become of set purpose something new; but what St. Jerome did in the fourth century did, none the less, constitute the first landmark; and he, well aware of his own place in a situation that promised so much for the future, made his own life story the final entry around the year 392.

To all this we must add his indefatigable correspondence. I have already spoken of the number of his letters; but one must also realize that most of them were veritable treatises. He sometimes dictated as much as a thousand lines a day.

Among his correspondents there was one we must specially mention—St. Augustine. When Jerome was in Rome, he was still simply a brilliant rhetorician, a believer in the teachings of the Manicheans; but since then he had been converted, had been baptized in 387, and, once more in his native land, North

Africa, was soon named Bishop of Hippo. North Africa was, we have seen, the home of a Christianity at once ardent and prosperous, and Jerome's writings were very influential there. But while many recognized his zeal, some were rather scandalized by the freedom with which he seemed, to their way of thinking, to treat Scripture. We find an echo of these criticisms in a letter that Augustine wrote him in 394. He encouraged him in translating Greek authors into Latin, but as regards the Bible, he added: "As for translating the sacred canonical books into Latin, I would rather you did not do it, except in the way you translated Job—that is, by using appropriate initials to indicate the places where your own translation differs from that of the Septuagint, whose authority is most important. Indeed I am astonished," he adds somewhat imprudently, "that anyone could still find anything in the Hebrew text which has escaped so many translators who know the language so well."

Augustine was a philosopher; all that mattered to him was the inner meaning of the texts. But Jerome was a scholar to whom historical exactitude was all the more important where the Word of God was concerned —especially since it had been so badly served by previous translators. Obviously their points of view were poles apart. But there is no question that in that age of inquiry, when heresies were multiplying and each making it possible to deepen some point of doctrine, no great synthesis could be made without the

indispensable foundation of sound texts on which to
base it.

One may wonder how Jerome would have received
the letter; fortunately it never reached him. But Augustine was not disheartened, and once again, in a letter
dating probably around 397, he once more attacked one
of Jerome's commentaries. This time the letter arrived,
but Jerome did not deign to reply. Yet another letter
along the same lines followed in 402. This time, Jerome
retorted in his usual way; we must not forget that he
was already a well known writer, a scholar whose learning was recognized as authoritative: "God preserve
me," he wrote, "from daring to interfere however little
in your works. I have enough to do to look after my
own. I have more to do than criticizing those of others.
Besides, you must know in your prudence that everyone agrees with his own ideas. It is childish vanity—
and what young people did in the past—to make accusations against well known men in order to gain a
reputation oneself. I am not foolish enough to take
offense if you put forward explanations different from
mine; you, then, should not do so if mine are the
opposite of yours."

The whole letter is in this style. Augustine can
hardly have been expecting this kind of reply, and
hastened to soothe his furious correspondent. He
wrote of his admiration for Jerome's work, but once
again expressed astonishment over the differences he
found between his translation and the Septuagint,

which had, up till then, been considered authoritative: "I would like you to be so good as to explain why in many places the Hebrew manuscripts differ from the Greek ones known as the Septuagint; for this version which has been so widely accepted, and was used by the Apostles, has no small authority."

Here we see Jerome's character in his refusal to be mollified: "Stop harassing an old man who seeks to be left alone in his solitude. If you want to show off your learning and display it, look for young men who are eloquent and well known. They say there are plenty of them in Rome. . . . If I speak in this way, it is not because I have found things to criticize in your works, for I have not taken time to read them. . . ."

This was enough to try anyone's patience. But not Augustine's. A little later, in the dispute over Origen, we find him strongly taking Jerome's part, and Jerome did, in the end, forget his rancor and make peace with the bishop of Hippo, especially since other preoccupations became more pressing.

For it would be wrong to imagine that Jerome's work was calmly carried on in a silent cell, protected from the troubles of the world outside by its enclosure. A large part of his work was actually produced by stimuli from without.

Many visitors indeed, always came to the hostelry that had been built for them in Bethlehem. Thus, in the year 395, a nun named Etheria came to stay there, and has left an account of her pilgrimage which is still famous—one of the oldest accounts of a pilgrimage to the Holy places, second only to that by an Aquitanian who had made the journey at the beginning of the fourth century. It appears that she too came from Aquitaine, and her account is permeated by her love of the Bible, which was illustrated for her by every step she took. She climbed Mount Horeb to see where the burning bush stood; on Mount Nebo she drank from a stream which she thought to be the one Moses had produced by striking the rock. Thus everywhere she stopped had its link with something in the Old Testament or the New, and the route she took was to be taken by pilgrims in the ages to come.

Also from Aquitaine came another visitor whose memory was much less pleasant to Jerome. A certain Vigilantius, a Spaniard, who had been an innkeeper before, and once converted, seemed drawn to the monastic life, presented himself one day at the Bethlehem monastery, sent by Paulinus of Nela. As we know, this latter, a Gaul from the Bordeaux region, and a pupil of Ausonius, had been moved by grace, and having been baptized in 390, had decided, along with his wife Teresa, to embrace the ascetic life; they gave away almost all their vast fortune and withdrew to the neighborhood of Barcelona, where Paulinus had become a priest. It must have been to learn more of the life of eastern monks that he had sent Vigilantius to St. Jerome. But it was not a happy choice. Vigilantius began by being tremendously friendly toward Jerome, but showed himself very limited, and criticized everything at random; Jerome was, of course, annoyed. Then one day, everyone in Bethlehem was wakened by earth tremors. Vigilantius behaved with a complete lack of courage; half-naked, he ran to take shelter in the cave of the Nativity, shaking with fear. The monks were not sparing of sarcasm, and shortly afterward, Vigilantius left Palestine and embarked for Egypt. But no sooner had he left, than he began to pour out calumnies against Jerome and his companions. In particular, he accused Jerome of holding the same heretical errors as Origen.

The accusation dropped into the midst of a tremendous dispute which kept arising to disturb the life of the Bethlehem monks and very nearly forced Jerome to leave this retreat he so loved, as he had fled from Chalcis and from Rome. The history of the Origenist controversy indeed filled a large part of his life. It was started by St. Epiphanius, the bishop of Salamis, who was in fact the protector and friend of St. Jerome. He decided, like so many others, to make a pilgrimage to Palestine and—around Easter, 393— sent ahead one of his companions, called Atarbius, bearing a kind of manifesto against Origen. Epiphanius had in fact found certain propositions in the writings of this great Scripture scholar that savored of heresy; this was no new suggestion, for it had long been thought in the eastern Church that some of Origen's theses were suspect: among others the idea that the creation of Adam and Eve's bodies was a result of the fall of their souls after sin; this would in effect mean a condemnation of matter—just as we find in Manicheism; and other propositions also were pinpointed by Epiphanius which seemed to make Origen one of the authors of the Arian heresy.

Faced with this evidence, Jerome, despite his great admiration for Origen, realized that he must agree in condemning him. We know how highly he valued him as an exegete, but this did not blind him to his errors. As he later, so wisely, said:

"I consider that one should read Origen from time to time, because of his learning, just as one reads Tertullian or Novation . . . and a number of other Greek ecclesiastical writers as well as Latin, accepting what is good in them, and leaving aside the rest."

But he also spoke his appreciation of the man and his work: "That Origen was a heretic does not signify. I do not deny that upon certain subjects he was. But he interpreted Scripture well; he has explained the obscurity of the prophets, and uncovered the mysteries of Old and New Testaments."

When Epiphanius himself came to Palestine, he was welcomed with open arms in Bethlehem; but in Jerusalem he was not: there the bishop John, and Jerome's old friend Rufinus of Aquileia refused to subscribe to the condemnation. Epiphanius was inflexible; he at once left Jerusalem, and returned to

Bethlehem, and a little later, took it upon himself to ordain Jerome's brother, Paulinian, who was, rightfully, a subject of the bishop of Jerusalem. This was enough to turn an awkward situation into an openly hostile one. Having returned to Cyprus, St. Epiphanius demanded that Bishop John should follow him in condemning Origen; he refused, and Epiphanius declared him a heretic, and commanded the monks in Bethlehem to reject all communion with him; John in his turn forbade Paulinian to exercise any priestly functions in his diocese. Jerome tried to pour oil on troubled waters by sending his brother to Cyprus, to Epiphanius' own diocese, but things went from bad to worse. He had been imprudent enough to translate the letter Epiphanius had sent John from Greek into Latin, upon the request of one of John's monks, Eusebius of Cremona, who did not know Greek. Then, as he had not foreseen, the letter was passed around; it eventually fell into the hands of John of Jerusalem and Rufinus, who examined it closely, found some differences between the Greek text and the Latin translation, and at once denounced Jerome for falsifying it. Jerome suspected Vigilantius, whom I mentioned earlier, of stealing the text; he declared that he was at liberty to give a Greek expression its Latin equivalent without translating it word for word, and further, that since it had not been intended for publication, he was not obliged to make his translation literal at the expense of style.

But John did not stop at words, or even at letters. He was a close friend of the Prefect of the Pretorium —another Rufinus, Rufinus of Aquitaine, whose power, in that period of confusion and the collapse of law in the Empire, was virtually limitless. He got him to make out an order exiling the monks of Bethlehem. The order was on the point of being carried out, when an unforeseen occurrence saved Jerome and his monasteries. A Goth, Stilicon, who dominated the West with his armies, detested the Prefect Rufinus, and arranged a conspiracy against him, which was successful. In the public circus, under the eyes of the crowd, on November 27, 395, the Goth troops surrounded Rufinus, and cut his throat with appalling butchery.

This did not make John of Jerusalem change his mind, however, and he had won the Patriarch of Alexandria, Theophilus, over to his cause. It was at this point that Jerome wrote a kind of apologia, called "Contra John of Jerusalem" in which, with his usual violence, he gave a summary of the whole affair, and set out clearly both the weakness and magnificence of Origen. Thereupon, Theophilus sent a circular letter to all the disputants, begging them to make peace. Jerome who, in spite of his impetuousness, longed deeply for peace, hastened to subscribe to it, and in 397, after a Mass celebrated in the basilica of the Holy Sepulchre, he was publicly reconciled with Rufinus of Aquileia.

Rufinus went back to the West, and immediately

set about publishing a translation of Origen, omitting
all the passages whose orthodoxy was open to question;
not content with this rather doubtful proceeding, he
gave his translation a preface in which he referred
freely to Jerome. We can imagine the anger with
which Jerome heard about this. Once again, his old
friend was compromising him in connection with
Origen! "These people do not want to be heretics without me!" he exclaimed. The letter he wrote in reply
was, as one would expect, very sharp, but it stated the
case with complete clarity. This time the quarrel
between the friends was final; Jerome had no further
reconciliation with Rufinus of Aquileia. A long controversy followed, in which each of the two former
friends set forth an apologia defending himself against
one who was now an enemy. Attacks followed from
both sides, and resulted at last in the calling of a
Council at which the Patriarch of Alexandria, Theophilus, was in violent opposition to the Archbishop of
Constantinople, John Chrysostom. The affair ended in
tragedy, with the Empress of Byzantium, Eudoxia, in-
tervening, to have John Chrysostom exiled, never again
to return to his see of Constantinople.

No less absorbing than the Origenist dispute was
the war against the Pelagian heresy, which reached its
high point around the year 415. Pelagius—whose real
name was Morgan—was a monk in Great Britain; for
this reason Jerome thought of him as "porridge-bellied"
—porridge being even then the staple food of the

country. Pious in many ways, he had gathered a large spiritual family, but he maintained certain errors—chief among them being that man could be purified without grace, thus minimizing the action of the sacraments. In fact, Pelagius more or less denied original sin. Jerome attacked him with his usual force, but was not able to convince the bishops who had come together at Diospolis to judge him.

He had returned, filled with bitterness, to Bethlehem when Pelagian monks, with unheard of audacity, actually made an armed attack on his monastery; a deacon was killed, buildings set on fire, and Jerome himself and his companions had to take refuge in the fortified towers which Paula had had the forethought to build. Pope Innocent, being informed of this, firmly condemned the action, as we would expect, urged the bishop, John of Jerusalem, to punish the culprits, and sent Jerome a letter of condolence. Thereupon, Jerome's action found support from the great bishop of Hippo, Augustine, who, in 418, convened a Council in Carthage at which all Pelagius' heresies were thoroughly examined, and solemnly condemned. The man himself was driven out of Palestine. Jerome's last letter was addressed to Augustine and his friend Alypius, and speaks of the joy of them all in seeing that, by their efforts, "a heresy is dead and buried."

It is clear that Jerome found his great consolations, amid so many sufferings and disputes, among his monks and nuns. Though so strict an ascetic, so intransigent a scholar that his writings give the impression of a man continually enraged, he was in fact a deeply sensitive being with a genius for friendship. He put his whole heart into his letters to Pammachius, to Paulinus of Nola, and, as well as his constant friends, Marcella, Paula, and Eustochium, there was Fabiola who, after a fairly worldly life, twice married and divorced, was converted, and having made a pilgrimage to the Holy Land, founded a hospital-cum-hospice for pilgrims and the poor in Ostia.

When his friendships were snatched from him by death his true feelings are given free rein. Jerome's long old age was marked by such period of mournings: Paula, first of all, died in 404 after a long illness, then Marcella in 411, and Eustochium finally at the end of 418. Jerome was to survive her by only a year. "The sudden death of the saintly and venerable virgin Eustochium," he wrote in one of his last letters, "has broken us all, and virtually changed our whole way of life. . . . All liveliness of mind and strength of body has left me."

Above all, we must remember that all this fever of activity, this constant vigilance over events and people, was going on against the darkest imaginable background. Few ages in history have been more troubled than these first years of the fifth century, which were so fruitful in Jerome's life and work. The attacks of the Huns were endangering the whole of the East, and spread terror even as far as Bethlehem. In July,

395, Jerome and his company prepared to return to the West. It was a moment when he was being fiercely attacked by John of Jerusalem, and everything seemed to fail him at once. From then on, receiving refugees was also to add to the problems of daily life in the Bethlehem communities.

This was but one shock among many; the last years of the Roman Empire were marked by the most frightful anarchy—the famous Roman "order" of Caesar Augustus was falling completely apart. All that remained of it were the barbarous amusements of the circus games (gladiators were still bleeding in combat at the end of the fourth century, and Jerome was among those who spoke in indignation against these horrors), the last traces of slavery, which was gradually dying out as Christianity spread, and an ever more crushing taxation, whereby small proprietors were often reduced to selling their lands and even their persons, to keep out of prison. Otherwise, it was the Army that ruled, making and unmaking emperors, while Visigoths, Goths, and Vandals overran the frontiers. In 410 the appalling news broke that the Barbarians had captured Rome.

This occurred exactly twenty years after one of the last of the great emperors, Theodosius, had proclaimed officially that Christianity was the imperial religion. It had been declared legal for no more than a century, and the moment when it was adopted by the civil power thus coincided with its fate once more seeming to hang in the balance. For it looked then as if all Christian life must end with the Empire. Alaric and the Visigoths who had seized the capital and spent three days sacking its glories, were Arians; many among the Barbarians were still pagans, and behind them flowed the hordes of Huns from Asia who threatened to submerge the Western world. We can imagine how hopeless it must have looked at the time.

In these circumstances, it was the Augustines and the Jeromes that the world needed. Such faith as theirs could see beyond appearances, could lean upon Christ in the absence of any human help. In *The City of God,* that magnificent work which was to be the inspiration of the Middle Ages, Augustine showed what relationship there was between the city of this world and that heavenly city which is the Christian's true home.

As for Jerome, all that he did was to reach its full flowering in the Middle Ages. His work survived the disasters of his own time to found a new age; it showed how the ancient civilization, wornout and dying, could be followed by a new kind of civilization, a new culture, founded this time on Holy Scripture, and formed by Christian teaching. For the canons of classical beauty, as expressed in the imposing colonnades of the pagan temples, in the cold perfection of academic statues, it substituted a new source of beauty, based not on the ideas of aesthetes or rhetoricians, but upon love, on a feeling for life, on the splendors of color, rhythm, and movement. Thus there was born that profoundly dynamic art of the great Roman and Gothic periods, the society that could do away with slavery by substituting technical improvements—such as the horse collar and the mill—which enabled man to harness nature, a society that also gave Christiandom the noble literary forms of the Middle Ages: the courtly love that inspired lyric poetry, the epic inspiration of the *chansons de geste,* and the wholly new theater that was born out of the Christian liturgy.

It was Jerome who shaped the language of all these things: the lovely medieval Latin of the Vulgate, from which the early romance languages were born. He mapped out in advance certain ways of life, by creating the monasteries in which that civilization was to develop; especially in the uncertain times of the High Middle Ages, the monasteries of women, many of which had abbesses worthy of Paula or Eustochium, played an important part in the transmission of culture. Finally, and supremely, with his passionate love of the Bible, he created the spirit that was to dominate that civilization.

When Jerome died, on September 30, 419, he could say with St. Paul: "I have fought the good fight, I have finished the course, I have kept the faith." With all his struggles, all his unremitting toil, he had in fact contributed to the preservation of orthodoxy, to the shedding of light amid the heresies that threatened the young Church; and this he did by his ardent seeking of the truth in Scripture, his patient research which he furthered by every human means possible. This scholar with his work of love shows that the "excellent way" of charity can be found only in truth. Even the anger and the rages with which he was sometimes reproached did not prevent the Church from declaring him a saint: even anger can sometimes be a manifestation of charity.

It is thought to have been after the Mohammedan invasion, in which the monasteries of Bethlehem and Jerusalem were destroyed, that his remains were taken to Rome, where they are still venerated in St. Mary Major—though there is only the vaguest tradition to guarantee their authenticity. Pope Boniface VIII, at the end of the thirteenth century, made him one of the four Doctors of the Western Church, with Augustine, Ambrose, and Gregory the Great.

To us he is the patron of exegetes, of translators, of all those concerned in historical studies, scholars, and philologists. It is comforting to think that the patron of so many formidable sciences was no humanist in an ivory tower, but a man wholeheartedly engaged in the events of his time, and in the best sense of the word, an enthusiast.

Bibliography

Jean STEINMANN, *Saint Jérôme*; Paris, 1958 (English translation, *St. Jerome and His Times*, Fides).

Paul MONCEAUX, *Saint Jérôme, sa jeunesse*; Paris, 1932.

P. ANTIN, *Essai sur saint Jérôme*; Paris, 1951.

For more serious study:

F. CAVALLERA, *Saint Jérôme, sa vie et son oeuvre*; Louvain and Paris, 1922, 2 volumes quarto.

J. LABOURT, *Saint Jérôme, Lettres*; Paris, 1949, 5 volumes octavo.

On St. Jerome's period:

DANIEL-ROPS, *L'Eglise des apôtres et des martyrs*;

Saint Jerome

Paris, 1948 (English translation by Audrey Butler, *Church of the Apostles and Martyrs*; New York, Dutton, 1960).

Paul MONCEAUX, *Histoire de la littérature latine chrétienne*; Paris, 1924.

P. de LABRIOLLE, *Histoire de la littérature latine chrétienne*; Paris, 1947.

Louis BRÉHIER, *L'Art chrétien*; Paris, 1928.